Christine Schirrmacher

The Sharia – Law and Order in Islam

The WEA Global Issues Series

Editors:

Bishop Efraim Tendero, Philippines
Secretary General, World Evangelical Alliance

Thomas Schirrmacher
Director, International Institute for Religious Liberty and Speaker for Human Rights of the World Evangelical Alliance

Volumes:

1. Thomas K. Johnson – Human Rights
2. Christine Schirrmacher – The Islamic View of Major Christian Teachings
3. Thomas Schirrmacher – May a Christian Go to Court?
4. Christine Schirrmacher – Islam and Society
5. Thomas Schirrmacher – The Persecution of Christians Concerns Us All
6. Christine Schirrmacher – Islam – An Introduction
7. Thomas K. Johnson – What Difference does the Trinity Make
8. Thomas Schirrmacher – Racism
9. Christof Sauer (ed.) – Bad Urach Statement
10. Christine Schirrmacher – The Sharia: Law and Order in Islam
11. Ken Gnanakan – Responsible Stewardship of God's Creation
12. Thomas Schirrmacher – Human Trafficking
13. Thomas Schirrmacher – Ethics of Leadership
14. Thomas Schirrmacher – Fundamentalism
15. Thomas Schirrmacher – Human Rights – Promise and Reality
16. Christine Schirrmacher – Political Islam – When Faith Turns Out to Be Politics
17. Thomas Schirrmacher, Thomas K. Johnson – Creation Care and Loving our Neighbors: Studies in Environmental Ethics
18. Thomas K. Johnson (Ed.) – Global Declarations on Freedom of Religion or Belief and Human Rights

"The WEA Global Issues Series is designed to provide thoughtful, practical, and biblical insights from an Evangelical Christian perspective into some of the greatest challenges we face in the world. I trust you will find this volume enriching and helpful in your life and Kingdom service."

Bishop Efraim Tendero, Secretary General, World Evangelical Alliance

Christine Schirrmacher

The Sharia
–
Law and Order in Islam

Translator: Richard McClary
Editor: Thomas K. Johnson
Editorial Assistant: Ruth Baldwin

The WEA Global Issues Series
Volume 10

Verlag für Kultur und Wissenschaft
Culture and Science Publ.
Dr. Thomas Schirrmacher
Bonn 2017

World Evangelical Alliance
Church Street Station, P.O. Box 3402
New York, NY 10008-3402 U.S.A.
Phone +[1] 212-233-3046
Fax +[1] 646-957-9218
www.worldevangelicals.org / wea@worldea.org

While this volume does not represent an "official" position of the World Evangelical Alliance we are distributing it to promote further serious study and reflection.

International Institute for Religious Freedom
of the World Evangelical Alliance
www.iirf.eu / info@iirf.eu

Friedrichstr. 38	PO Box 535	32, Ebenezer Place
2nd Floor	Edgemead 7407	Dehiwela
53111 Bonn	Cape Town	(Colombo)
Germany	South Africa	Sri Lanka

2nd edition 2017
© Copyright 2013 by
Verlag für Kultur und Wissenschaft
(Culture and Science Publ.)
Prof. Dr. Thomas Schirrmacher
Friedrichstraße 38, 53111 Bonn, Germany
Fax +49 / 228 / 9650389
www.vkwonline.de / info@vkwonline.de

ISBN 978-3-86269-042-8 / ISSN 1867-7320

Printed in Germany

Cover design:
BoD Verlagsservice Beese, Friedensallee 44, 22765 Hamburg, Germany

Production:
CPI Books / Buch Bücher.de GmbH, 96158 Birkach
www.cpi-print.de / info.birkach@cpi-print.de

Publisher's Distribution:
Hänssler Verlag / IC-Medienhaus
71087 Holzgerlingen, Germany, Tel. +49 / 7031/7414-177 Fax -119
www.haenssler.de / www.icmedienhaus.de
Individual sales: www.vkwonline.com

The WEA Global Issues Series is sponsored by:

Gebende Hände gGmbH / Giving Hands International
Adenauerallee 11 • D-53111 Bonn • www.giving-hands.de

Martin Bucer Seminary
European Theological School and Research Institutes
Bonn – Zurich – Innsbruck – Prague – Istanbul
www.bucer.eu

Contents

Editor's foreword 7
Preface: What Is the Sharia? 8
    Why are law and religion so tightly woven together in Islam? 9
    The concept of the Sharia 10
    The Sharia – the 'way to the watering place' – only theoretically God's law? 13
    From which sources did the Sharia arise? 15
    What do the claims of the Sharia mean in practice? 19
    Old sources – new interpretations 20
    The absence of a highest teaching authority 21
    What are the characteristics of the Sharia? 22
    The Sharia – a workable legal system? 23

The Main Contents of the Sharia 25
    Marital and family law 25
    Islamic criminal law 36

The Sharia in Europe? 47
    The migration of Muslims to Germany 47
    The current Sharia discussion in Europe 52
    Literature 63

About the Author 69
    Published by the Author 69
    Biography 73

Editor's foreword

Centuries ago the West might have been indifferent to the question of how the Islamic legal system operates. However, in times of globalization we can no longer afford to ignore the legal approach that is valid in Islamic countries and at least theoretically of importance to one billion Muslims. For a long time now, we have been affected by the repercussions in our everyday life, as well as through global politics, to the facts that our neighbors are Muslims and that in German courts the question of the validity of Islamic legal practice is being debated.

Law in European societies is a mixture of Christian ethics and history, Greco-Roman civilization, and the achievements of the Enlightenment and democracy. None of these three roots can help us to truly understand the legal systems of other cultures, such as the Islamic or Chinese culture. These societies function too differently, whether regarding the family, the relationship of state and religion, or the structure of shame and guilt. For this reason we have to be taken by the hand so that we can be introduced to this foreign world in a concise manner.

There are only a handful of specialists who know the Sharia from its original sources and have studied the various forms, past and present, that the Sharia has taken in different countries. And out of this group there are in turn only a few individuals who are in a position to summarize their specialized knowledge briefly and understandably – compactly – so that it can be used by the individual who wants to understand his neighbor or classify a newspaper article. The author of this volume has demonstrated in reference books and talks at scholarly symposia how thoroughly and in which varied manner she has occupied herself with the meaning of the Sharia around the world. At the same time, she has shown in books such as *A Small Dictionary About Islamic Families* (in German only: *Kleines Lexikon zur islamischen Familie*) that it is possible to make specialized knowledge understandable so that it helps everyone who has something to do with people with Muslim background on a daily basis.

Thomas Schirrmacher

Preface: What Is the Sharia?

A few years ago most people in Germany would have had to invest some effort to look up the word *Sharia*. Recently, however, and in particular since terrorist attacks on the World Trade Center in New York in 2001, the concept shows up increasingly in the press and other media reports. Has that helped to clear up what the concept means?

Sharia is often used as a buzzword to describe the influence of Islam in Germany. However, not everything relating to Islam at the same time has to do with the Sharia. Rather, much belongs in the category of societal development, which resulted from the immigration of guest workers beginning in the 1960s. For a long time this either went unnoticed or was consciously ignored. The situation has definitely changed now that there are around 3.2 to 3.4 million Muslims who permanently live in Germany (with a tendency for further growth) and between 16 and 20 million Muslims in Western Europe. As a result, the topic of the Sharia does not just occupy Near East experts and scholars of Islam. Rather, it actually concerns everyone who lives in Germany and for that matter in Europe.

The subject matter is of particular importance for the legal area. Legal questions over the past two decades have not just had to do with making legal decisions relating to calls to prayer made over loudspeakers, to mosques and minarets, or to a teacher's wearing a headscarf. Rather, legal questions have also had to do with allowing the absence of anesthesia when slaughtering animals, honor killings, arranged marriages and exemptions from class trips, school sport activities, and biology class. In Arabic countries women often inherit only half of what men do, and their testimony in court is valid only in limited manner or not at all. When charged with adultery, they are punished more severely. In many countries they can do nothing against their husband's marrying a second or a third time, nor can they undertake any action against being cast out or regarding their children's being taken from them after a divorce.

All of what I have just mentioned has to do with the Sharia, without even opening a law book or a Sharia legal text to try and find these rules. The Sharia is not something that has been poured into book form as a legal text and which contains all sorts of rules. On the other hand, however, it is not an indefinable, indistinct entity, which exists only in theory. It is on the one hand interpretable and thereby principally flexible, and on the other hand its roots are from the time of the seventh to the tenth centuries A.D.

Many feminists and human rights activists emphasize that Islam has nothing to do with the oppression of women and that the Sharia would not envision discrimination. Rather, this viewpoint has to do with a misogynistic interpretation. So, in its pure form is the Sharia a tool for equality and a refuge of freedom that has only become an instrument of oppression in the hands of political and religious elites through the misuse of power and misinterpretation?

In a way everyone can understand, this book lays out what the Sharia is, how it originally developed, how it is interpreted today, which subject areas it covers, which subject areas it does not address, and what this means for Christians and Muslims living side by side in Europe.

What the Sharia is not:

- A complete catalog of laws
- A book of statutes that can be purchased and placed on a bookshelf
- A printed collection of laws which a person could use, for instance, to look up Sharia-specific penalties for adultery, murder, and theft.

What the Sharia is:

- An ideal of God's law, which up to the present day the majority of Muslims, at least in theory, hold to be unchangingly valid
- An interpreted collection of rules, regulations, and instructions stemming from several centuries. Neither these rules, regulations, and instructions nor their interpretations are summarized in any one particular place.
- A catalogue of commands addressing all areas of life.

Why are law and religion so tightly woven together in Islam?

When Mohammed, as the founder of Islam, preached belief in the one God, Allah, and each person's responsibility after death in his hometown of Mecca around 610 A.D., he did this primarily as a warning about judgment and as an admonisher who called upon Arab tribes to leave their polytheism and to submit to the one God. From 610 A.D. to 622 A.D., Mohammed remained someone who proclaimed ethical values and norms which were in part true innovations and contrasted with old Arabian customary law, and in part compromises with traditional law.

In the first twelve years that Mohammed proclaimed monotheistic faith, he encountered many adversaries, even enemies, such that the situation for him in the city of his birth, Mecca, became increasingly threatening. When he finally came under so much pressure due to a boycott, and his adherents and supporters remained low in number and without significant influence, he left for the neighboring city of Medina in 622 A.D. This year could be considered the actual birth of Islam.

In Medina Mohammed found a completely different situation. He gained influence not only as a religious preacher, but also as a lawgiver and a military leader.[1] He led several wars of attack and defense against the three Jewish tribes located there as well as against several Arabian tribes. He also created numerous legal regulations for ordering the civic life of the first Muslim communities in Mecca.

For this reason there are religious as well as legal aspects in the Koran that we above all encounter in Medina. They have to do with regulations for divine service and social regulations, which are interwoven with each other. Faith, society, and politics as well (i.e., above all with respect to conducting war and battling enemies of the young religious community) represent a unity in early Islam, which was symbolized by the person of Mohammed as lawgiver, prophet, and military leader. Islamic law thereby united religious as well as social aspects.

The way of exercising religion – above all the obligation placed upon everyone to follow the five pillars of Islam (profession of faith, ritual prayer, fasting, almsgiving, and Hajj or pilgrimage to Mecca) – is not a question of private activities tied to individual choice. Rather, as is the case with questions of inheritance and family law, they are elements of the Sharia as is criminal law. As a result, insofar as the treatment of concrete legal questions is concerned, there should theoretically be agreement among Arab states which expressly consider the Sharia to be significant or even among states such as Sudan, Yemen, and Libya, which consider the Sharia to be their sole legal basis. However, this is not at all the case.

The concept of the Sharia

The notion of the Sharia is often conveyed as "Islamic jurisprudence" or "Islamic law." This is, however, partially inapplicable, because it suggests

---

[1] In contrast to this widely received notion stands the minority conception that Mohammed never intended the founding of a nation: compare Bernard G. Weiss, *The Spirit of Islamic Law* (The University of Georgia Press: Athens, Georgia, 1998), p. 3.

that we are dealing with a corpus of clearly defined laws that have been established by a lawgiving body. This is not the case.

The Sharia encompasses comprehensive legal guidelines for all areas of life that are justified by Islam. This means the entirety of the commands of Allah, as they are laid down in the Koran and Islamic tradition and interpreted by leading theologians. 'Leading' means the foremost theologians from the seventh to tenth centuries A.D. In individual cases there is, among theologians, strong disagreement as to what the Koran precisely seeks to regulate. For example, does the Koran teach polygamy, or does it oppose it? There are different opinions found in the writings of the theologians. Furthermore, there are numerous cases in which tradition formulates guidelines deviating from the Koran. This means that there cannot be such a thing as *the* Sharia as a composed set of laws.

The Sharia equally treats the vertical as well as the horizontal relationships of every person. It provides directions for ethical behavior within the family and within society (e.g., in matters relating to business, inheritance, foundation law, marital law, and criminal law), but it also regulates the exercise of faith and religious actions such as the many guidelines relating to prayer, fasting, and pilgrimage. Just as little as the course of daily ritual prayer is left to the individual's discretion, so little does personal discretion apply to the necessary clauses of a marriage agreement, which have to be fulfilled in order to make a marriage legally 'valid.' Maurits Berger appropriately characterizes the Sharia as:

"... a set of rules for everything that can happen in life to a person, for all his behavior and his entire way of life. It concerns itself equally with correct behavior in the bathroom as well as on the battlefield, and in the marketplace as well as in the mosque."[2]

Little has changed with respect to the unalterable authority of the Sharia as God's law since its inception in the early days of Islam, although of course there are critical Muslim voices emphatically calling for a reform of the Sharia. Nevertheless, there are Sharia norms which had already developed in the first centuries of Islam. These norms were taken up in the legislation of countries influenced by Islam, albeit in differing degrees.

Also, in cases where this was only partially the case, the Sharia exerts significant influence due to its claim to be the actual valid provider of di-

---

[2] Maurits S. Berger, "The Shari'a and Legal Pluralism: The Example of Syria" in Baudouin Dupret, Maurits Berger, Laila al-Zwaini, *Legal Pluralism in the Arab World*, Arab and Islamic Laws Series, vol. 18 (Kluwer Law International: The Hague, 1999), 113-124, here p. 114.

vine law and the fact that it provides societal norms for all behavior. One might mostly hold to the laws of the state (as, for example, with Turkey's laws regarding monogamy), but the Sharia in its overarching claim is never essentially relativized or, from either the side of theology or politics, ever placed into question. For this reason the Sharia is for many people – among them many immigrants to Western countries – the actual framework for their life and faith. A consequence is, for example, that polygamy is still very often practiced according to the Sharia. This is particularly true in rural areas of Turkey. Polygamy also occurs because it corresponds to the 'feeling' of a right to follow the higher order of the Sharia over all earthly law.

In relatively secularized Syria, the influence of the Sharia on the sense of right and wrong is also recognized in a practical manner. In Syria there are numerous so-called 'Sharia groups' which teach the *application* of the Sharia to students. This occurs via personal lessons by a religious leader as a complement to the 'actual' study of law at university. The application comes by putting the teaching into practice as much as possible in one's own life and in thinking about legal matters. What is thereby created is a mindset that lets it appear to a student who has had such informal training that Sharia norms are the 'actual' framework. At the same time, the leaders of these Sharia groups, the sheiks, also exert public teaching influence in the media, at universities, or as preachers at mosques and as muftis (individuals who provide legal opinions). In this way, next to a rather moderate "state Islam," a conservative and orthodox Islam is simultaneously disseminated. Indeed it does not speak from the highest political positions (as, for instance, is the case in Iran) but it cuts across many areas of society in exerting noticeable influence. Through this and other channels of communication, occupation with and application of the Sharia play a much larger role in social life than would initially be supposed by comparing Syrian legislation with Sharia norms.[3]

For this reason, disdain for the practical meaning of the Sharia would lead in the wrong direction, even though in numerous countries and in many areas of life it is not at all (or only in extremely limited fashion) put into practice by law. In everyday life the Sharia's norms are found in texts handed down that are quoted at births, marriages, funerals, and festivities, among other situations. The same applies to tradition and to the sense of right and wrong that are also so influenced. The reason for this is as follows:

---

[3] See the depiction from his own observations in Damascus, ibid., pp. 115ff.

Preface: What Is the Sharia?

"... many Arabic countries ... (are), to an extent difficult to understand, permeated by a traditional law according to the Sharia ..., so that the Muslims submitting to it first of all see all actions and expressions of life to be graduated forms of what is allowed or viewed as depraved by or before God. It is the religious privilege of the Sharia to regulate collective and individual convictions and behavioral expectations and is for the analytical grasp of a Western scholar difficult to reconstruct. It is not, for instance, a disconnected yet comprehensible area with norms of law and morality, nor is it merely a 'rational' set of ethics, such as is characteristic for the more or less positivistic legal orders in the Continental European realm, with its separation of church and state and the separation of politics and morality."[4]

The Sharia – the 'way to the watering place' – only theoretically God's law?

The concept of Sharia is only found once in the Koran (Sura 45:18), and in that verse it is not used to designate a legal system. Rather, it means "rite" or "way." The concept originally meant "the way to the watering place," because *"salvation, which God offers one to acquire, resembles a watering place in the desert."*[5] The concept of the "way" points to a central motive of the Koran: man, who is not basically evil or sinful, yet weak and able to be influenced, has to be led upon the right path by God. This way of formulating 'guidance' arises again and again throughout the text of the Koran, and as early as Sura 1 it is used with the phrase: *"Keep us on the right path. The path of those upon whom Thou hast bestowed favors"* (Sura 1:5, 6). This guidance occurs through God's legal ordinances. Whoever does not pay attention to them will be "those upon whom Thy wrath is brought down ... [and] those who go astray" (1:6). The concept of "Islam" means "submission" or "devotion": Whoever recognizes the authority of God's commands and holds to them, submits to God and will be rightly led by him.

Therefore, the concept of Sharia in the Koran itself does not have the meaning of an elaborate legal system. It was only through a long period of development, which began in approximately the eighth century A.D. and

---

[4] Birgit Krawietz, *Die Hurma: Schariarechtlicher Schutz vor Eingriffen in die körperliche Unversehrtheit nach arabischen Fatwas des 20. Jahrhunderts* (Duncker & Humblot: Berlin, 1991), p. 77.

[5] Tilman Nagel, *Das islamische Recht: Eine Einführung* (WVA-Verlag Skulima: Westhofen, 2001), p. 4.

found a preliminary end in the tenth century, that the concept of Sharia became a synonym for 'God's law.'

Because it is a matter of God's law, the Sharia is seen to be a perfect ordinance, bringing peace and justice to every society, since God is a God of justice. A homogeneous society, operating under his perfect legal system, is viewed as a synonym for a peaceful society. For this reason there is a connection between "Islam" and "peace."

Since the Sharia was given by God himself, it is principally unable to be reformed or disputed. To critique the Sharia means to place human considerations above the law of God. It is also, therefore, senseless and wrong, because at the end of all time Islam will be the only existing religion, and the Sharia will be set up over all people. This is at least the official claim of conservative theology. There are also liberal alternative viewpoints, but they all have little influence.

Because the Sharia contains norms for all areas of life, there are as such no secular areas that are independent of religion. According to the self understanding of the Sharia, by which God revealed his eternal law to man, it is not a question of whether to relativize its claim or practice it only partially. Rather, the question is how to find the appropriate application in order to configure life in this world in a manner pleasing to God and as preparation for paradise in the next world. This is in turn not viewed as a conviction of some orthodox outsiders, but rather it should be seen as the widely accepted position within Islamic theology. This is the case even if everyday life of a lot of people might look different. The Sharia counts as worldly as well as sacred law, divine in its origin, and claiming to address not only religious but also worldly areas of life as well.

Combining affiliation with Islam with a fundamental criticism of the Sharia is on the one hand problematic, because, at least in core Islamic countries, there is neither true religious freedom nor freedom of expression. Therefore, there is no critical public discussion as to the rights of a holistic claim by the Islamic religion and its representatives. On the other hand, the alliance between law and religion creates practical problems with respect to critical reflection on the claims of the Sharia. This is because *"to confess this religion without affirming the law in its entirety and as an indubitable and ever valid standard for all of one's lifestyle is impossible; this is due to the fact that the law is a significant portion of the Islamic message of salvation."*[6]

---

[6] Tilman Nagel, op. cit., p. 3.

From which sources did the Sharia arise?

In spite of this general claim of the Sharia to seek to regulate all areas of a person's life, it may not be assumed that the Sharia is a codified law book that is comparable to the German Civil Law Code. On the contrary, it is a set of regulations based on multiple sources which are interpretable and were never compiled in a single work.

The Sharia is based concretely upon three sources: the Koran, tradition (i.e., stories about Mohammed and his companions as well as interpretations, in particular up until the tenth century A.D., by early Islamic lawyers and theologians and largely recognized as normative. Up until that time, four different 'schools of law,' or legal traditions, arose in the Sunnite realm (the Hanbali, Hanafi, Maliki, and Shafi'i schools) as well as at least one Shi'ite[7] school. Admittedly the deviations – at least in the Sunnite realm – range only slightly, so that the differences between the teachings of the legal schools are not really fundamental.

The Koran

The first source of the Sharia is the Koran; all of its legal regulations are components of the Sharia. Certainly the Koran is not first and foremost a book of law, since around only 10 percent of its text concerns itself with legal questions. Furthermore, many of the topics are only treated in a fragmentary manner, and none of the legal questions are treated systematically and exhaustively. What one finds is above all case examples, which is also easily explained when one assumes that the Koran to a certain degree records Mohammed's legal decisions in his first congregation.

Regarding several questions of law, such as, for example, property law, the Koran only gives scant details. Regarding other areas of law, such as marital law and family law, it gives more concrete opinions. Family law solely based on the Koran's provisions would not, however, be able to be formulated by virtue of the Koran's brief remarks.

Tradition

The second source of the Sharia is the Islamic tradition, or the *hadith* (Arabic for tradition, report), "*a type of Islamic tradition and addendum to*

---

[7] Regarding the development of Twelve-Imam Shiite Law, see Harald Löschner, *Die Dogmatischen Grundlagen des Shi'itischen Rechts*. Erlanger Juristische Abhandlungen vol. 9 (Cologne, 1971).

*the Koran."*⁸ Among this is above all a number of reports by and about Mohammed, his family, and his companions which were collected and written down a significant time after Mohammed's death. In addition to events from Mohammed's time, tradition contains numerous detailed directions relating to the practice of faith and treats a number of legal questions. This circumstance is surely a consequence of concrete legal cases that arose and which were brought to Mohammed and, after Mohammed's death, his successors.

While with respect to the non-legal area covered by tradition Muslim believers are only called upon to copy Mohammed's 'habits' (Arabic *sunna*) and follow him as a role model, following the legal regulations in the tradition is an absolute duty. For this reason, when tradition says that Mohammed had a beard, then this counts as 'sunna' (a habit that is to be copied) for men in order to emulate Mohammed's position as a role model. In so doing, a believer demonstrates his *"love for the prophet."*⁹ Whoever does not do this, however, is not guilty of sin or of a criminal act, because the action does not have to do with a law or a legally binding regulation.

The situation is different when it comes to legal questions: Where the tradition regarding legal questions takes a firm stand (e.g., divorce law), it has as much authority as the text of the Koran itself, and according to the predominant opinion it is preferred over the Koran insofar as it makes alternative and substantial statements. This was how ash-Shafi'i (767-820 A.D.), who was surely the most notable Muslim legal practitioner of early Islam and is known as the "father of Islamic jurisprudence,"¹⁰ advocated interpreting the Koran by tradition (and not vice versa!).¹¹ Ash-Shafi'i viewed Mohammed's legal judgments – that are more frequently recorded in tradition – as divinely inspired and for that reason binding for all time for Islamic society.¹² Since individual reports that are more frequently handed down in everyday life are generally speaking better known as cultural assets than the text of the Koran, which in its specific language is not easily understood, what has been handed down as tradition exerts significant influence over the general sense of right and wrong.

---

[8] Isam Kamel Salem. *Islam und Völkerrecht: Das Völkerrecht in der islamischen Weltanschauung* (Express Edition: Berlin, 1984), p. 33.

[9] Ahmad Hasan, *The Principles of Islamic Jurisprudence*, vol. 1. (Islamic Research Institute, International Islamic University: Islamabad, 1983), p. 85.

[10] Noel Coulson, *A History of Islamic Law* (Edinburgh University Press: Edinburgh, 1994), p. 61.

[11] Joseph Schacht, *An Introduction to Islamic Law* (Clarendon Press: Oxford, 1996), p. 47.

[12] Coulson, op. cit, p. 56.

Preface: What Is the Sharia?

For the sake of completeness it has to be mentioned that when it comes to 'tradition' we are not speaking of a single text, but rather – in the Sunnite realm – about six extensive collections by various authors taken to be authoritative and containing tens of thousands of individual texts on numerous topics. These, in turn, have differences among themselves and even indicate contradictory differences with respect to legal statements.

In what has been handed down there are numerous regulatory statutes for the sometimes brief instructions found in the Koran regarding, for instance, marital and family law. In what is considered tradition it is rather unmistakably and repeatedly reported that Mohammed had apostates to Islam condemned to death, while the Koran itself does not contain any such report. It is chiefly on the basis of what has been handed down as part of tradition that the Sharia's demand for the death sentence for apostates (converts) is largely undisputed among theologians of all four Sunnite legal schools and of the Shi'ite legal school as well. In practice, cases of apostasy are very seldom negotiated before a court. This changes nothing, however, with respect to the principal legal validity and acceptance of this article of the Sharia.

Whoever does not follow the legal regulations of tradition commits a sin as well as a penal offense (e.g., by marrying two sisters and thereby entering into a marriage that is forbidden according to the Sharia). Even when the Koran sets out that it takes two confirming testimonies by women to balance out one testimony by a man (Sura 2:282), and many Muslims find this to be unjust and not in line with prevailing circumstances, this principle still has found its way into the law codes of several Islamic countries, e.g., in Iran. Although the Sharia has not been completely put into practice in any of these countries, it cannot be overlooked that regulations anchored in source texts are not without significance for legislation in particular countries today.

If, therefore, according to the majority understanding the Koran likewise allows polygamy as it does the authority of the husband over the wife – under certain circumstances to the point of her measured beating (4:34) – then this is not primarily a culturally determined seventh-century A.D. opinion that needs to be revised. Rather, according to the opinion of a still increasing number of Muslims (though not all), since it reflects divine commands it should be reflected in current legislation in Muslim countries. In the recent past there has been a frequently brought forward demand, that it is not the Sharia that needs to be modernized but rather modernity that needs to be oriented towards the Sharia.[13]

Women's and human rights organizations in Islamic countries protest vehemently against such a type of 'timeless,' historically uncritical, and general application of a (Koran) text from the seventh century A.D. The difficulty consists, however, in the fact that with an overall lack of coming to terms historico-critically with Islamic history and theology, the call for a modern interpretation is quickly met with an accusation of 'heresy' or 'unbelief', with reformers being discredited in the eyes of many traditionalists as 'un-Islamic.'

The interpretation of theology

The Koran and tradition that have been handed down are only concretely comprehensible and applicable after they have been interpreted by Muslim theologians. The floodgates to interpretation, however, are not open with respect to a diversity of opinions. The legal compendia of significant theologians and legal practitioners from the days of early Islam are first and foremost what leads the way up to the modern age.

When Mohammed died in 632 A.D., neither the text of the Koran nor the texts belonging to tradition were present in their entirety. Rather, at best, there were fragments. The "habits" (Arabic *sunna*) of the prophet, which later made their way into the texts belonging to tradition, certainly were an important factor in the first decades after Mohammed's death for the practical organization of the Muslim community. Supposedly most of the texts of the Koran and the reports about Mohammed were initially passed down orally. The majority of the Koran texts seem to have been orally preserved and recited by transmitters or Mohammed's companions. Written legal texts with 'Islamic' legal regulations hardly existed at the dawn of Islam in written form. Rather, they became part of customary law by being passed down orally.

We can draw from the Koran that the Old Arabic customary law was in part abolished by Mohammed: Mohammed revoked the apparent practice (from days prior to Islam) of burying newborn girls out of a fear of falling into poverty (Sura 17:31) and partially modified old regulations. Thus, for example, polygamy or the right to blood vengeance was limited but not completely abolished (Sura 4:3; 2:178-179).

---

[13] Lecturer for criminal law and criminal procedure in the department for Sharia and law at the United Arab Emirates University, Butti Sultan Butti Ali Al-Muhairi,. "Islamisation and Modernisation within the UAE Penal Law: Shari'a in the Modern Era in *Arab Law Quarterly*, vol. 11, Jan 1996-Dec 1996, pp. 34-49, here p. 34.

What do the claims of the Sharia mean in practice?

As early as the first decades after Mohammed's death, Islam spread all the way to Spain and to Central Asia. Not only did a functioning administration have to be quickly established in these places, but an Islamic legal system as well. In the first decades after Mohammed's death, this certainly did not yet exist. Up until the end of the eighth century A.D. – which is to say a period of around 150 years after Mohammed's death – there was still no proper Islamic jurisprudence. For that reason one could not yet speak of *"a uniform Sunni law"* at the dawn of Islam.[14] It was not until the beginning of the tenth century that Islamic law became a set of regulations in which it was also defined how new cases could be resolved according to generally valid principles.[15]

Due to the fact that as early as the time of the first four caliphs (632-661 A.D.) Islamic conquests occurred at a swift pace, the necessity soon arose to establish a legal system in the newly conquered Islamic areas and to resolve many concrete questions pertaining to, above all, marital and family law. In the first decades, only Koran texts and ancestral customary law were available. Unfortunately the sparse amount of source material does not allow us to come to a complete history of the development of Islamic law. However, it can be concluded that out of the circles of the first scribes in those early decades the 'ulama' emerged, a legal discussion circle of scholars (Arabic *fuqaha'*). This was a *"group of religiously oriented men who reviewed several legal judgments by governors and judges."*[16] This occurred primarily in Medina, Kufa,[17] Mecca, Damascus, and Basra. It was there that discussion about practical matters of law was held, so that what began to develop was a form of Islamic jurisprudence (Arabic *fiqh*). Out of this there arose 'legal schools' (traditions of interpretation), from which four Sunni Islam schools developed by the tenth century A.D. They are the

---

[14] Adel El-Baradie, *Gottes-Recht und Menschen-Recht* (Nomos: Baden-Baden, 1983), p. 75.

[15] Auch Wael B. Hallaq, *A History of Islamic Legal Theories: An Introduction to Sunni Usul Al-Fiqh* (Cambridge University Press: Cambridge, 1997), p. 3.

[16] W. Montgomery Watt; Alford T. Welch. *Der Islam I. Mohammed und die Frühzeit, Islamisches Recht, Religiöses Leben. Die Religionen der Menschheit.* vol. 25,1. (W. Kohlhammer: Stuttgart), p. 240.

[17] Kufa and Medina could be viewed as the centers of early Islamic law, especially as three of the four Sunni legal schools originated there (the Hanbali school in Kufa and the Maliki and Shafi'i schools in Medina); furthermore, Kufa played a significant role in the development of Shi'ite law: Bernard G. Weiss. *The Spirit of Islamic Law* (The University of Georgia Press: Athens, Georgia, 1998), p. 9.

Hanafi, Hanbali, Shafi'i, und Maliki schools. There must have been other schools as well that simply did not endure.

The most pressing question that had to be answered by these legal scholars was how legal questions could be decided when there was no example or guideline in the Koran or in that which had been handed down as tradition. There was no doubt among the four named Sunni legal schools that the Koran and tradition were to be viewed as the first sources for the course of justice. However, since ash-Shafi'i (d. 820 A.D.), what were also considered sources of justice were agreement among scholars with respect to a particular question (Arabic *ijma'*) and an analogous conclusion (Arabic *qiyas*).

Therefore, the Sharia has its roots in certain legal rulings during the seventh and eighth centuries from Arabian tribal society that had no formally drafted political system. Overall, our knowledge of the concept of law and related practices found in pre-Islamic tribal society is rather scant. What we do know is that the records and development of Islamic law came to a sort of standstill by the end of the tenth century. That had to do with putting the major sources of the Sharia into written form: the text of the Koran, which had been completely put into written form during the sixth and seventh centuries; tradition, of which earliest written forms exist beginning in the eighth or ninth century; as well as their interpretation, which was set down in the time period up to the tenth century. After the tenth century, a further development of Islamic law was frequently called for by way of an independent legal course of justice (Arabic *ijtihad*), but it was never generally accepted. However, in a certain manner this always took place given the standard of interpretation.

Old sources – new interpretations

This means that the main features of Islamic law stretch back to the tenth century A.D. and have their roots in the seventh century, that is to say, at the time of Mohammed's life. Several aspects are actually older, because Mohammed picked up on customary law that he found when he proclaimed Islam.[18] On the one hand, then, Islamic law is an age-old legal tradition, the preservation and handing down of which are inseparable from the preservation of religion. On the other hand, Sharia law is not actually an unvarying congealed block. In practice it had to be interpreted and applied, which is to say it was always being interpreted anew.

---

[18] O. Spies; E. Pritsch, „Klassisches Islamisches Recht. 1. Wesen des Islamischen Rechts" in *Handbuch der Orientalistik*, Sect. 1. Suppl. vol. 3. *Orientalisches Recht* (Leiden, 1964), p. 223.

What this means concretely is that to a certain degree conservative understandings regarding the veiling of women or legal discrimination of women goes back to time-honored Sharia norms or were justified by them. Liberal interpretations, which call for more rights for women and minorities in Islamic countries, also similarly invoke the same Sharia norms in an attempt to reconcile the Sharia's moral norms with the demands of modernity. This is done because there is officially no critique of the Sharia. The door for a liberal interpretation, therefore, is opened, not by a fundamental critique of the Sharia, but rather by justifying modernity with the Sharia.

Turkey is a notable exception: as early as 1926, in the course of the founding of the Turkish Republic, Kemal Atatürk aligned family law with the Swiss Civil Code and abolished the Sharia as a basis for law. For this reason, one does not find a legal orientation in Turkey that is oriented towards the Sharia, while at the same time the legal sensibilities of many people are anchored in this religious law.

Since the Sharia is not a body of laws with formulated norms, but rather repeatedly reinterpreted and reformulated into concrete laws, there is indeed the opportunity for the development and extension of rights for women and minorities. In this way in many countries influenced by Islamic there has been, for example, an extension of the right to divorce granted to women with reference to a more just interpretation of the Sharia. At the same time, the possibility for men to practice polygamy has been restricted using the same justification.

The absence of a highest teaching authority

Norms from the Sharia cannot be given for Islam once and for all for the simple fact that in Sunni Islam there is no highest teaching authority or office that could set down which interpretation comes under the framework of the Sharia and which is not in line with it. For this reason, the Sharia, on the one hand, continues to have the claim of being the eternally valid law of God. Simultaneously, due to the quite different interpretations that are made in practice, there have been curtailments in its reach. On the basis of different interpretations there can be no unified Sharia-based legislation that finds agreement among all countries shaped by Islam. Indeed the Sharia remains the indisputable ideal. Simultaneously, however, due to a lack of sources, there is highly limited knowledge regarding concrete details about living conditions at Mohammed's time. Thus, among Muslim scholars, the question of how a complete implementation of the Sharia could occur can hardly be answered in a way that is uniform and practically relevant.

As a legal system the Sharia is at the same time concrete and interpretable. It can be shown to be hard-set or flexible. In concrete form it is specifically followed since legal guidelines regarding marital and family law are in a certain sense clearly defined in the Koran and in tradition. In the early days of Islam these norms were interpreted in a path-breaking manner by leading theologians and legal practitioners. Hence there is a certain stiffness to the system. On the other hand, the Sharia remains interpretable because it can be implemented only by interpretation and application. Therefore, it offers some latitude for a certain spectrum of opinion as long as such opinion can be substantiated with the Sharia itself.

Since the interpretation of legal guidelines and their application as concrete legal provisions differ significantly in parts, there are no unified legal texts cast as the 'Sharia.' There is a certain basic corpus of legal concepts which can be derived from the Koran and tradition. Furthermore, there are a number of different interpretations from numerous legal schools as well as particular and significantly varying conclusions that have been drawn for local legislation in individual countries.

What are the characteristics of the Sharia?

The Sharia can, then, be seen as concrete law and imprecise law at the same time, on the one hand as time-honored norms with application in modernity and as officially binding in Islam, and on the other hand still applied in very much a piecemeal manner:

Features of the Sharia

- The Sharia grew 'from the bottom up' out of practical questions and not by being implemented as a rule book 'from the top down'. It is seen to have been *"worked out in a manner completely independent of all worldly ruling powers."*[19]
- The Sharia is an ideal that has never been completely applied in legal practice. It has to do with a model or conception of divine and indisputable law that is viewed to have 'completely' applied at Mohammed's time. By returning to the 'complete' application of the Sharia as called for by some groups, all people are supposed to experience peace, and Muslims are to regain a leading role in the world.
- The ideal of the Sharia stands in opposition to the historical fact that in the early days of Islam there was no 'Sharia' that existed without gaps

---

[19] Isam Kamel Salem, *Islam und Völkerrecht: Das Völkerrecht in der islamischen Weltanschauung* (Express Edition: Berlin, 1984), p. 27.

and that encompassed all fields of law. In its beginnings the Sharia developed out of the legal regulations of Mohammed and the four caliphs on the basis of the concrete necessity for legal conditions in the newly conquered Islamic areas.

- The theoretical claim of the Sharia on the individual is high. At the same time, for the layperson the Sharia as such is not directly accessible. Knowledge of it and application is reserved for Sharia scholars, because complicated particular explanations, for example regarding Islamic inheritance law, are only locatable in the works of Islamic legal practitioners and theologians. The layperson requires an expert in Arabic, theology, and law, because only such a person can give an answer to technical questions from normative writings according to the rules of his own legal school.

The Sharia – a workable legal system?

The Sharia is not codified law, and it has at no time and in no place ever been completely put into practice. It has always remained an ideal, and therefore the question can be asked whether it – and this applies all the more in the twenty-first century – could ever be put into practice in its entirety. This question also arises due to the many ways it can be interpreted and our sketchy knowledge about the conditions of early Islam. Nevertheless, the Sharia is on the other hand not an ambiguous quantity, the contents of which cannot be determined whatsoever, or a collection of unclear regulations where any interpretation would be possible. Specifically in the cases of marital law, family law, and in criminal law as well, the Koran and tradition contain comparatively detailed instructions that limit the interpretive possibilities. The practice of theology in the early days of Islam resulted in records of these interpretations in comprehensive commentaries, which traditional theology follows in fundamental legal questions – specifically in marital and family law.

In Islamic countries up into the nineteenth century there was no codification of law. The Ottoman Family Code, dated October 25, 1917, was the first law book on family law in the Islamic world that was based on the Sharia.[20] In the course of building nation states in the twentieth century,

---

[20] Hans-Georg Ebert, „Wider die Schließung des ‚Tores des igtihad:' Zur Reform der sari'a am Beispiel des Familien- und Erbrechts" in *Orient* 43 (2002), pp. 365-381, here p. 368.

most other countries shaped by Islam produced their own legal codes[21] that are more or less strongly based on the Sharia.

Present-day law in countries shaped by Islam is a mixture of Koranic guidelines (and this in turn is a mixture of old Arabian customary law[22] profoundly acting upon Islam and the supposed earlier legal elements such as that of Persian-Sassanian, Jewish and Roman law[23]), guidelines given in tradition, interpretations of notable legal practitioners and theologians, but also European legal elements that above all found their expression in Arabic countries in the course of colonial times.

As a result, wherever individual countries seek a return to and full application of the Sharia, this is more a wish than reality. Sudan (1983), Iran (1979/1982-83), Pakistan (1979), several of Nigeria's northern states (beginning in 2000), Yemen und Libya (both in 1994) as well as the province of Aceh in Indonesia (2002) have all expressed this precise wish. What is mostly meant with such statements is a closer orientation towards Islamic marital and family law, a stronger control regarding dress codes for women, the application of corporal punishment such as lashings, stoning for adultery and fornication and even cutting off parts of or all the limb of the body. In particular cases these actions have been applied in the countries named, whereby the question admittedly has to be asked whether the motivation truly has to do with a 'complete' enforcement of the Sharia or whether it has primarily to do with a political power game among various interest groups intended to make concessions to the Islamic opposition as well as a demonstration to the outside – with the consequence of arbitrarily adopted legal norms used on defenseless and mostly uneducated people who have no societal recourse or status.

---

[21] An overview of marriage and family legislation in several Arabic countries of Northern Africa and the Middle East is given by Dawoud Sudqi El Alami, *The Marriage Contract in Islamic Law in the Shari'ah and Personal Status Laws of Egypt and Morocco*, Arab and Islamic Laws Series (London, 1992).

[22] Also Kamel Salem. *Islam und Völkerrecht: Das Völkerrecht in der islamischen Weltanschauung* (Express Edition: Berlin, 1984), p. 17.

[23] Comp. the discussion with Ulrike Mitter, *Das frühislamische Patronat: Eine Untersuchung zur Rolle von fremden Elementen bei der Entwicklung des islamischen Rechts* (Ergon: Würzburg, 2006), pp. 16-18.

The Main Contents of the Sharia

Marital and family law

Marital and family law are considered the core of the Sharia.[24] To a certain extent today, the Sharia has legal force in all countries shaped by Islam, including parts of Africa and Southeast Asia. In the core Islamic countries (with the exception of Turkey), the Sharia is a significant or even sole basis for civil status law and at the same time a foundation for the administration of justice in civil litigation. A purely secular administration of justice, uncoupled from religious norms, therefore does not exist with respect to marital and family issues. As a result, Sharia guidelines also form the legal backdrop for current-day marital and family law. Stated alternatively, current-day family law in Islamic countries is neither comprehensible nor imaginable without guidelines from the Sharia.[25]

Because an official critique of the Sharia does not exist, it is basically questions of interpretation that are discussed with respect to the Sharia. On the one hand, with the increasingly clearly visible Islamization in many countries, there are growing numbers of conservative voices calling for a return to the Sharia in issues relating to marital and family law. They view existing legal structures as a compromise with Western notions of law and demand a renunciation of all 'non-Islamic' regulations which in part stem from colonial times. This demand is in part also heard from conservative women's organizations. On the other hand, quite a few countries in past years have extended the rights of women and improved their legal standing. Simultaneously, out of consideration for the conservative and Islamist following, what have been mostly cautiously introduced as Sharia regulatory reforms will remain operative only in a limited fashion as long as the

---

[24] An overview of the statutory provisions of Islamic marital law is, for example, provided by Jamal J. Nasir, *The Islamic Law of Personal Status* (Graham & Trotman: London, 1986); a comparison between the individual Sunni legal schools and Shi'ite conceptions is offered by Syed Ameer Ali, *Mahommedan Law*. 2 vols. (Kitab Bhavan: New Dehli, 1986); an overview of the individual relevant specifications of the Islamic penal code has been given by Abdul Qader 'Oud Shaheed, *Criminal Law of Islam*. 2 vols. (International Islamic Publishers: New Delhi, 1991).

[25] For example, the largely unquestioned juridical impact of legal marriages. "Legal" marriages are those that do not contradict corresponding Sharia norms. The impacts of legal marriages can be compared at, for instance, M. A. Qureishi, *Muslim Law of Marriage, Divorce and Maintenance* (Deep & Deep Publ.: New Delhi, 1992), pp. 87-88, 93-94.

sacrosanct character of the Sharia is not challenged and the standard of a tribal society and its way of life in the seventh century basically not disputed.

On the one hand, the strict principles relating to marital and family law coming from the Koran and tradition are nowhere completely put into practice. On the other hand, the Sharia continues to be basically judged as the only system on earth that gives husband and wife freedom, justice, and dignity. As a result, a partial orientation towards the Sharia and its family law is a reality in those countries which have made curtailments in the strict interpretation of the Koran and texts handed down and belonging to tradition.

Advancements in Islamic family law

Although the classical interpretation of marital and family law narrowly defines women's room to maneuver, the situation of women in individual countries is definitely varied. Some countries have improved the position of women in recent years with respect to divorce and child custody law and have raised the minimum age at which boys and girls can marry. Other countries – in particular those on the Arabian Peninsula – do not have a family legal code, with the result that legal action taken by women and relating to marital and family issues (e.g., the desire for a divorce) are practically hopeless.

The topic of religion is not the sole topic at issue in justifying the limitation on women's rights in Islamic countries. Disadvantageous power structures and deeply rooted traditions, closely tied with religious values, often make it impossible for women to make independent occupational and private choices in daily life. Where theoretically Islam would provide freedom for women, it is in practice frequently impossible to claim these freedoms because the societal reality and the desire to preserve tradition do not allow it. For example, Islamic tradition advocates that both women and men attain knowledge and education. What is generally considered in the Near East to be respectable behavior of women, however, de facto denies women's attending university or upper level schools. This is the case inasmuch as, for example, long distances or intensive contact with male teachers, lecturers, or fellow students are involved that could damage the honor of the family. Because culture and religious tradition provide for gender segregation and there is an unconditional necessity for young women to safeguard their good reputation, the notion many families have is that this weighs far more than the benefit of attaining an education. Furthermore, the interest of the family and society – their reputation and their standing – come before individual interest.

According to Western notions, the oppression of women in Islam is indeed above all seen in externals, such as the headscarf. However, the actual discrimination is found at another point: while the headscarf, according to the overwhelming majority opinion, neither forbids attending university nor following a career, and even young Muslims with headscarves are frequently highly educated and self-confident advocates of their faith, the actual discrimination of Muslim women occurs in the legal area.

Expansion of women's rights

It should not be overlooked that in recent decades quite a number of countries shaped by Islam have made legal changes in family law that have the result of improving the position of women. Admittedly, however, these legal changes serve as advantages for women in urban settings. The tendency in many locations is to raise the minimum age for marriage (instead of the earlier widely common marrying of daughters at the onset of puberty) as well as to increase state registration of marriages (instead of the customary and non-public execution of a contract between two families), which make it not so easy to divorce by simply casting off a wife. The tendency is also to move in the direction of a limitation on polygamy by requiring judicial approval for a second marriage, coupled with a disclosure of the existing financial circumstances (instead of what had prior been left to the individual: the decision to marry a second or third time) and the requirement for an attempt at reconciliation before granting a legal divorce (instead of traditional divorce proceedings, which involve the husband's informal thrice repeated verbalization of the phrase relating to divorce: "I divorce you").

An extension of the legally acceptable reasons for divorce in the case of proceedings initiated by the wife (instead of the traditional notion that a divorce by the wife was only rarely possible) is recognizable in numerous countries. There is likewise a principle improvement in the regulation of child custody such that after divorce the mother is no longer basically excluded from child rearing and from contact to the children (instead of granting the father the sole exercise of child rearing beginning with the age of seven in the case of boys and the age of nine in the case of girls).

In other countries shaped by Islam, however, the opposite development can be observed: in the return to Islam and its legal principles there is a 'cleansing' of legislation considered to be European legal elements from the colonial past as well as the claim of an alleged 'complete introduction of the Sharia.' In recent years in countries such as Nigeria, Iran, or Sudan there have been show trials – in particular concerning adultery – as a public demonstration of the reintroduction of the Sharia. Of course not only religious reasons play a role here. Rather, there are complex societal as well as political reasons that play a role. It is apparent that one is not dealing with a case conforming to the Sharia when, for example, one would actually have to convict the father of the child born out of wedlock as well. Rather, it has more to do with going before the world at large and the Islamist opposition to make an example of a member of a minority who has no rights or is from an underprivileged social class.

Indeed in theory the body of regulations from the Sharia that addresses the topic of marriage and the family is relatively uniform – excluding any different notions stemming from the individual schools of law – but in practice the regulations from the Sharia are, however, handled very differently from country to country and as a result can have very different repercussions on Muslim women's legal and societal situation. In addition to this, there is the important factor of local cultural norms that are lived out, which are rooted in part in Islam and in part in pre-Islamic times and are now justified by Islam and inseparably woven together with it.

Also, the degree of piety of individual families plays an important role as well as the question of whether a woman and her relatives live in a rural or an urban setting. An urban, and at best affluent, family environment that is open to education and progress offers a woman completely different opportunities for development and maneuvering than a rural, traditional, and economically less developed environment that in many cases leaves a woman with no options with respect to her marriage or career.

The complex problem relating to women's "obedience"

Muslim apologetics has always emphasized the equal rights of women in Islam. For one thing the equality of the woman – according to Muslim apologetics – is derived from the Koranic creation narrative (Sura 39:6; 49:13), which explains how God created human beings as man and woman without making a difference in rank between the two. Furthermore, men and women are equally bound to hold to the commandments of Islam, first and foremost the 'five pillars.' Men and women are "created ... from a single being" (Sura 4:1) and are to be "guardians" (Sura 9:71) or friends to each other. Both are equally promised paradise if they humbly "submit" (Sura 33:35) to God and do "good whether male or female and ... [as] a believer" (Sura 16:97). Mohammed, according to Muslim apologetics, improved the position of women and bestowed true dignity and esteem upon them.

Regardless of the creation account, where initially man and woman are undoubtedly placed upon the same rung, in another place the Koran – and more so what has been handed down as Islamic tradition – justifies explicit legal discrimination against women. The verse in the Koran that is of great importance in this connection is Sura 4:34: *"Men are the maintainers of women because Allah has made some of them to excel others and because they spend out of their property; the good women are therefore obedient...."* Similar to this is a portion of Sura 2:228: *"... the men are a degree above them ..."* Muslim theologians frequently comment traditionally on these verses as follows: *"Men and women do not have the same value as people."*[26] The renowned Koran interpreter Ibn Kathir expounds Sura 4:34 with the words *"Men are superior to women and a man is better than a woman."*[27]

As a result, from Sura 4:34 in particular, there are two baselines relating to classical Islamic marital law that have been derived and that are viewed as a guarantee of justice and stability in family life: The domination of the man over the woman is justified with the fact that God has placed man over the woman (Sura 2:228) as well as with the fact that men "spend" for their wives (Sura 4:34). This spending refers to the largely corresponding point of view that men have the duty of supporting their wives, while wives "submit" to their husbands and are to be "obedient" (Sura 4:34). This obedience is first and foremost related to sexuality, because the man receives the right to sexual relations when the contract is concluded and financial support is provided (comp. Sura 2:223; 2:187).

This does not mean, of course, that in each individual Muslim marriage the basis of obedience and (one-sided) support is the case. The urban educated elite in particular view this traditional understanding in a more differentiated manner and in practice aim at and achieve equal partnerships. That does not change anything about the fact that even today freedom to make decisions is unachievable for a large proportion of women in traditional environments. On the other hand, in order to achieve equal rights women practically always need the permission or support of their male family members and without them can only achieve limited independence. Where the economic conditions allow, it can be the case that family relations are configured less strictly. This is also to say that such relations are more urban and Western, if family relations do not break apart in case of controversial attitudes.

Still, the two pillars of classical Islamic marital law remain, as before, 'support' and '(sexual) obedience.' This will not basically change as long

---

[26] P. Newton and M. Rafiqul Haqq, *The Place of Women in Pure Islam*, (Caney, 1994/3), p. 2.

[27] Ibn Kathir, op. cit.

as these values are substantiated with the Sharia and the Sharia's general claim as divine law for earthly concerns is not generally called into question. According to the traditional and predominantly held understanding, at the time of marriage the wife receives the right to support that refers to the daily means of sustenance (food, clothing and adequate housing) and according to the Maliki legal school also extends to the medical care of the wife in the case of illness.

Support and obedience are mutually dependent: if a husband fails to meet his obligations for support, his wife receives the right, so to speak, to be disobedient.[28] If she is disobedient (e.g., by leaving the house against the husband's will[29] due to employment), the husband can stop providing financial support. With respect to the question of obedience the basic issue is not so much a cultural question of the way one marriage or another is conducted, but rather it has to do with a legally binding commitment which the woman enters into at the time of marriage on the basis of the Sharia.[30]

This basis of Islamic marital rights where supremacy and subordination are present has a number of consequences that have an impact on the entire range of Islamic marital, divorce, and custody laws.

Where is it apparent that men are legally favored and women discriminated against?

Regarding witness law: According to Sura 2:282, the testimony of a man can only be offset by two women, because one woman can make a mistake. Tradition contains – in addition to many positive statements about women, in particular mothers – several texts attributing lower intellectual abilities to women. Since tradition has also never been exposed to basic historico-critical evaluation by official theology, this leads to a situation where numerous Muslim theologians attribute greater emotional instability, irrationality and limited insight into intellectual affairs to women "on the

---

[28] Regarding the marital legal definition of 'undutiful,' in particular by leaving the home on one's own authority (to go to work, for instance), comp. Lynn Welchman, *Beyond the Code*: *Muslim Family Law and the Shari'a Judiciary in the Palestinian West Bank.* (Kluwer Law Int.: The Hague, 2000), p. 222ff.

[29] Only the Hanbali legal school exclusively recognizes leaving the home against the will of the husband as 'rebellious' (Arabic *nashiza*) behavior; for the three remaining Sunni legal schools it is also rebellious (undutiful) if the wife remains at home but refuses to participate in marital sexual relations: David Pearl. *A Textbook on Muslim Law* (Croom Helm: London, 1979), p. 65.

[30] Shahla Haeri also emphasizes this. "Divorce in Contemporary Iran" in Chibli Mallat, Jane Connors (eds.), *Islamic Family Law* (Graham & Trotman: London, 1993), pp. 55-69, here p. 61.

basis of their natural constitution." For example, *"Women are under the mastery of their feelings, whereas men follow their reason."*[31] Muslim apologetics do not see slighting the witness of women as oppression. On the contrary, Islam requires no more from women than they are in a position to accomplish on the basis of biological facts. *"The intellectual superiority of a man over a woman ... is simply predefined by nature."*[32] Koran verses such as Sura 2:282 (which have not been worked through historico-critically and relativized in their intensity for the present), tradition that devalues women, and theologians who emphasize the already mentioned inferior abilities of women, all produce a societal climate that fosters disdain for and slighting of women, even when in contrast there are many self-confident and self-determined women. The existence of self-determined women alone – above all in urban areas – will, however, hardly bring about sweeping societal change if the foundations of the Sharia are not shaken.

Laws relating to corporal punishment: In addition to the inequalities in marital law, there is also the well known 'punishment verse' in the Koran, which according to widely accepted opinion gives the husband an educational and disciplinary right over his wife: "and (as to) those on whose part you fear desertion, admonish them, and leave them alone in the sleeping-places and beat them ..." (Sura 4:34). Indeed tradition calls men at the same time to treat their wives well. Numerous theologians also emphasize that a woman may never be fiercely hit or hit in the face (indeed that no 'hitting' at all is meant) – at least not to a degree that an injury is suffered, but rather that only a symbolic action is meant in order to humble them (e.g., with a "toothbrush").[33] Other law practitioners, however, name a 'cane' or a 'whip' as a legitimate instrument of punishment that a man may use on his wife.[34] Islamic apologists emphasize that to strike is a means of last resort if a wife is unmanageable and if there is no other way to bring 'peace' into the household. Since the husband is more rational and is the head of the family, it rests upon him to maintain order and to end rebellion and strife – by force, in the case of an emergency. The following from Mohammed has been passed down in tradition: *"The prophet said: Do not strike the maidservants of God. Since 'Umar came [the second caliph, who*

---

[31] Murtada Mutahhari, *The Rights of Women in Islam* (Tehran, 1981), p. 182 with reference to a non-Muslim psychologist.

[32] Ibid.

[33] Also in a legal commentary for the British Indies dated 1940: David Pearl, Werner Menski, *Muslim Family Law* (Sweet & Maxwell: London 1998/3), p. 187.

[34] Abdul Qader 'Oud Shaheed. *Criminal Law of Islam*, 2 vols. (International Islamic Publishers: New Delhi, 1991), here vol. 2, p. 235.

ruled from 633 to 644 A.D.] and said: 'O sent one from God, the wives rebel against their husbands.' So he allowed him to strike her."[35]

The question also arises at this point as to how these ordinances might look in practice. Naturally it is not the case that all Muslim women are beaten by their husbands. On the other hand it cannot be maintained that violence against women is solely a Muslim problem. By no means. Furthermore, Muslim jurisprudence dealt early on with the question of true abuse of women. The Maliki legal school expressly allows the wife a divorce on the basis of cruelty,[36] and numerous countries have de facto provided women the opportunity to divorce for this reason. True abuse, therefore, is also condemned in Islam.

On the other hand, a divorce on account of abuse is mostly only possible if the woman has the financial resources for the support of her family, the financing of education, and for providing herself prospects for the time after divorce. The husband – with the exception of a few months in the case of pregnancy – does not have to provide financially. In addition, mentioning the possibility of punishment – and strictly speaking even the instruction to use it – offered by the Koran and supported by tradition, provides for a societal conscience that views punishment as a religiously legitimate way to guide a wife. This has an influence on the societal climate. A wife who is beaten will also frequently be confronted in her surroundings with the attitude that she herself must have been the cause for being beaten and for leading her husband to resort to such means. In this way the victim is made out to be the culprit.

In divorce law: Divorce law based in the Koran and tradition discriminates against women in favor of men: The traditional formula "I divorce you," for which the husband does not have to name any reasons, is in many countries not sufficient according to national laws. However, it continues to be practiced and is in many cases recognized by society. Even in the case where the husband has to go through divorce via court proceedings, it is still easier for him than for her. She always has to – if she even has the possibility of pursuing a divorce – bring a court action and cannot simply declare divorce. She additionally needs sound reasons as proof for the husband's misconduct so that a divorce can be granted. Above all, those reasons that are considered misconduct are the ones the Sharia stipulates, such as, for example, imprisonment, neglect or violence. Simultaneously a di-

---

[35] Quoted according to Adel-Theodor Khoury. *So sprach der Prophet: Worte aus der islamischen Überlieferung*, (Gütersloh, 1988), p. 268.

[36] Comp. David Pearl, *A Textbook on Muslim Law*. (Croom Helm: London, 1979), p. 109.

vorce can leave a woman socially stigmatized and in an economically desperate situation.

A 'revocable' divorce can be granted only to a man, whereby he verbalizes the divorce phrase only one time and can leave his wife in a state of uncertainty between divorce and marriage for weeks or months. The decision of whether the husband retracts the divorce at the end of the third month at the latest and continues in the marriage, or allows the last day on which he can take her back to pass by and considers the woman to be divorced from him, is something that is left completely to him. Admittedly in recent decades various countries have made it more difficult for the husband to divorce by using the simple formula for divorce. This has been done by allowing divorce papers to be produced only after one or two demonstrated attempts at reconciliation or after a mediator has been appointed.

In child custody law: According to traditional opinion based on the Sharia, a pair's children after divorce always belong to the man, because he is the sole legal guardian and can make all decisions. Even when the children remain with the mother until the end of their time of infancy, which is what the Sharia actually allows for, this right can be taken from her or exchanged against the right to get a divorce from her husband. While classical Islamic law views the mother only as a temporary custodian for boys until the age of seven, and for girls until the age of nine, many Islamic countries have raised these ages and allow the mother to now have the care of boys until the age of fifteen and the care of girls until the age of eighteen and sometimes even until her marriage. Admittedly, in a society where legal priority is so strongly in favor of the father, it is not seldom the case that ways and means are found to take these rights from the mother.

In marriage: If marriage occurs within the traditional framework, which at any rate still today accounts for the majority of marriages in non-urban areas, many women are married off by their guardians, frequently also without having their own voice in the choice of a marriage partner. Quite a few countries have at least taken the legal measure of raising the minimum age for girls and boys to sixteen and eighteen, respectively. Large families are suffering signs of disintegration in urban areas, where social control is becoming less stringent and 'love marriages' are occurring more frequently.

Nevertheless: Only a portion of Muslim women are in the position of making their own choices with respect to general prospects in their lives as well as regarding their husbands. A majority are married off by their families, in that their parents negotiate for the bride and make the final decision. The marriage contract, which in particular includes the amount of the dowry, is generally negotiated, not by the woman but rather by her family.

In what has been handed down as Islamic tradition, there are definite statements to the effect that a woman is not to be married against her will. A woman's silence, however, can be taken as approval, and if the family agrees and an appropriate candidate as groom is found, women can only decline the intended marriage once or not at all – or alternatively choose between numerous cousins. In actual fact the woman is not 'forced' into marriage, but according to a Western understanding she also would not be thought to have freely initiated the marriage.

In polygamy: Discrimination against women of course also includes polygamy, which principally always opens the possibility for a man to enter into an additional marriage (Sura 4:3) and can degrade the woman to a second or third wife. Exceptions are Tunisia and Turkey. Women are not allowed to practice polygamy. It is indeed the case that numerous countries influenced by Islam have made multiple marriages more difficult and require approval either from the first wife (e.g., in Egypt) or also from the local authorities (as in Pakistan[37]) or by a court (as in Pakistan[38]) or by a qadi (in Iraq, for instance[39]) before the marriage is concluded. In addition, Shi'ites practice the 'limited time marriage' (or 'indulgence' marriage), which is a type of additional marriage that extends beyond the allowed four wives for a limited period of time and can be entered into without the approval of the wife (or wives). Only a small number of marriages in countries shaped by Islam are polygamous, not, however, because they are forbidden or are considered to be principally scandalous. Polygamy requires certain financial preconditions, since each wife has a claim to being cared for and to being given her own living quarters.

In inheritance law: Women are clearly discriminated against in inheritance law. They always receive what amounts to one-half of that which a male family member in the same position would be awarded. By the way, it deserves mention that Muslim inheritance law is exceedingly complex.

---

[37] Comp. the relevant specifications regarding the consummation of a plural marital relationship in Pakistan by David Pearl. "Three Decades of Executive, Legislative and Judicial Amendments to Islamic Family Law in Pakistan" in Chibli Mallat, Jane Connors (eds.), *Islamic Family Law* (Graham & Trotman: London, 1993), pp. 321-337, here p. 322.

[38] Hans-Georg Ebert, „Zur Anwendung der sari'a in Libyen," in *ZDMG* 143/1993, pp. 362-370, here p. 367.

[39] According to David Pearl. *A Textbook on Muslim Law*. (Croom Helm: London, 1979), p. 71.

With respect to family honor: Finally, family, society and Near Eastern Muslim culture assign women a subordinate position by recommending or even ordering women to hold to manners of modesty and decency by preferably remaining at home. To avoid leaving home prevents having contact with men who are not relatives which could thereby give rise to immorality. Again in this case it is not that the Sharia would explicitly express the order that a woman not be allowed to leave her house at all, because the majority of Muslim women do this and many women also have occupations. On the other hand, tradition contains numerous dicta from early Islamic authorities, which in a rather disparaging manner state that a society is morally endangered when a woman leaves the house and that as a potential temptress of a man would just as well remain at home. These old texts influence societal thought, even though individual families draw various conclusions from them.

It is the woman who has to veil herself, and she is responsible for upholding public morality and the reputation of her own family. Her behavior is strongly controlled on the basis of the aforementioned norms. Indeed in theory both the Koran and tradition foresee the same punishment for the man as well as the woman in the case of fornication or adultery. However, in practice, men are under less control prior to and even once married and encounter less mistrust. As a result, they are by far granted greater room to maneuver, since the woman alone is considered the preserver of family honor and her behavior, and not that of the husband, dishonors the family.

Nevertheless, from a Muslim point of view this legal and universally held higher social higher ranking of men is by all means reconciled with the principle of equality which Islamic human rights declarations formulate for men and women. This is due to the fact that women are admittedly of equal value but are not equally created. A woman has the same dignity but not the same rights. The dissimilarity between men and women is expressed in the different assignment of tasks which are predefined by pregnancy and birth. Islamic marital law promotes, not oppression but rather the protection of women – such is the form Muslim apologetics takes.

Islamic women's movements call for augmented rights and have been able to achieve several successes that however in part have been impeded by the increasing present-day resistance from Islamic powers. However, as long as the Sharia's formative influence on society and consciousness basically remains untouched, the extension of women's rights in Islamic countries will be limited.

Islamic criminal law

In addition to marital and family law, Islamic criminal law accounts for the second focus of the Sharia and, furthermore, is one of the topics where there is the greatest difference when contrasted with Western notions of human rights. On the one hand, nowhere in countries shaped by Islam has Islamic criminal law truly been comprehensively put into practice. There are curtailments everywhere, and in many cases criminal law as it is now described has in practice not been applied at all. Very early on, Islamic jurisprudence found many ways around the law – so-called 'legal tricks' – in order not to infringe upon its theoretical validity and at the same time not to act according to it and use severe punishments. Today only a few of these punishments are carried out, and when so, then only in a truly small number of cases. But even here the same thing applies, and that is that deeply rooted Sharia norms influence the general consciousness, and today Islamic groups are attempting to more strongly awaken this consciousness and to present the reminder that God's law is the actual frame of reference for social life.

Islamic criminal law is mostly broken down into three sections: capital offenses, offenses of retaliation, and discretionary offenses. All offenses always contain a legal as well as a moral aspect. Islamic criminal law is for that reason not only a system for the definition of certain offenses and their punishment, but rather simultaneously a moral doctrine to teach and reform people, warn them about punishment and thereby to generally inhibit evil in society.[40]

Comparably few offenses and their designated penalty are named in the Koran. For that reason, no criminal law can be established upon the basis of the Koran. In several questions the Koran breaks from customary Arabic law, and in several questions it modifies it, for example when it allows limited retaliation in the case of murder and manslaughter. In addition there is a large spectrum of offenses for which revenge is largely left to the discretion of the relevant legal bodies.

What are capital offenses?

Capital offenses or restrictive ordinances are those relatively few offenses that the Koran or tradition threatens with a defined punishment. They

---

[40] In particular, Nagaty Sanad emphasizes the moral authority of the Sharia. *The Theory of Crime and Criminal Responsibility in Islamic Law: Shari'a.* (Office of International Criminal Justice, The University of Illinois at Chicago: Chicago, 1991), p. 49ff.

are considered capital offenses because the offender transgresses a border (Arabic *hadd*). Whoever commits a capital offense does not break human law but breaches God's law,[41] that is to say, that a border or boundary is overstepped. A court proceeding on account of a capital offense cannot be warded off by an out-of-court settlement, and the punishment may be neither exacerbated nor reduced. Rather, the punishment that has to be carried out must be administered precisely as it is prescribed in the Koran or received tradition.

Capital Offenses

1. Adultery and fornication: extramarital sex that is conducted without coercion by individuals who are of the age of consent, mentally healthy, and not married to each other or who are single. According to Sura 24:2-3, the Koran threatens those who are unmarried and impure with 100 lashes with a whip. In the case of married people, tradition calls for the death penalty. If the woman is unmarried and the man married, the woman is to be confined to home "*until death takes them away or Allah opens some way for them*" (Sura 4:15). If the man is unmarried and the woman married, he should be banished for a year and the woman is to receive 100 lashes with a whip.

2. False accusation of fornication or adultery (slander): According to Sura 24:2-3, false accusation of fornication or adultery (slander) is to be punished with 80 lashes with a whip. This regulation, as a supposed protection from slander, can also be used against the victim of rape if a woman brings a complaint but cannot produce any evidence. In this case evidence is exclusively four male eyewitnesses or a guilty plea. Since such evidence is rarely to be brought in the case of rape, there is the threat of counter-complaint for slander associated with fornication after the victim's complaint has been filed. The woman can be flogged and would become a victim for a second time. This is not simply a theoretical issue. In Pakistan there have frequently been such cases, and there is an actual report from the state of Zamfara in Nigeria dated September 2000.[42]

---

[41] B. Carra de Vaux, J. Schacht, *Hadd* in *Encyclopedia of Islam*. vol. 3 (Leiden, 1986), p. 20.

[42] The pregnant, unmarried Bariya Ibrahim Magazu, whose age was officially given to be 17, while unofficial sources places her age at 13, was convicted in the State of Zamfara, Nigeria in September 2000 to receive 180 lashings with a whip: 100 lashings for fornication and 80 lashings for slander, since she pressed charges against three men for rape. The sentence was later reduced, because she withdrew the court action. Peters, Ruud, *The Reintroduction of Islamic Criminal Law in*

> **3. Theft:** Sura 5:33, 38 as well as tradition call for the amputation of the right hand for the first such offense and in the case of a repeated offense the amputation of the left foot. By finding numerous excuses to prevent theft from being designated as such (e.g., pick pocketing, theft as a result of desperation, theft of one's own property by failure to provide compensation, and much else), Islamic jurisprudence has in practice found several ways to avoid this stiff penalty. Furthermore, the Hanbali legal school recognizes the 'legal trick' that the accused swears that the stolen goods belong to him in order to avoid amputation.[43]
>
> **4. Highway and robbery homicide:** According to many legal scholars, highway robbery (without theft or murder) should be punished with imprisonment or banishment. Highway robbery calls for the amputation of the right hand and the left foot. If the killing of an individual occurs in addition to highway robbery, the offender receives the death penalty.
>
> **5. The consumption of wine:** (Arabic *shrub al-hamr*) or generally the consumption of all intoxicating drinks. This frequently also includes all types of drugs. Tradition calls for 40 lashes with a whip (other traditions say 80) as a punishment for consuming wine.

Tradition, and not the Koran, additionally names homosexuality and rape as capital crimes. Admittedly, the sentences for these crimes are subject to controversy in discussions among Muslim theologians. Legal practitioners call for the death penalty in these cases, while others rank homosexuality among those offenses that can be punished at the discretion of the judge. According to the majority opinion of all four legal schools, falling away from Islam calls for the death penalty, although the Koran only specifically threatens those who turn their backs on Islam with a penalty in the afterlife. In this life only tradition clearly calls for the death penalty. Liberal positions, as for instance held by Abdullahi Ahmed an-Na'im, Professor for International Law at Emory University in the United States, who was influenced by the Sudanese theologian Mahmud Mohammad Taha (executed in 1985),[44] denies the justification of the death penalty. If a convert to the Christian faith is killed by the individual's family or other members of society, however, although the individual was acquitted by a court, it is

---

Northern Nigeria: A Study conducted on behalf of the European Commission (Lagos, 2001), p. 20.

[43] Adel El Baradie, *Gottes-Recht und Menschenrecht: Grundlagenprobleme der islamischen Strafrechtslehre* (Baden-Baden), p. 115.

[44] Comp. the description of his position in Lorenz Müller, *Islam und Menschenrechte: Sunnitische Muslime zwischen Islamismus, Säkularismus und Modernismus.* (Deutsches Orient-Institut: Hamburg, 1996), p. 241.

a demonstration of just how deeply the sense of justice is influenced by the norms of the Sharia.

The sentence for all capital offenses is indeed extremely hard, but the conditions for a conviction are also difficult to meet: either by confession or a testimony by two credible male eyewitnesses, and in fact, in the case of adultery and fornication, four male eyewitnesses are required. A confession has to be voluntarily made and the individual admitting guilt has to be of age, mentally healthy, and has to have acted willfully.[45] Muslim legal practitioners have repeatedly emphasized that the accused, in the case of doubt, should not be punished with the capital punishments, since in the case of doubt Mohammed spoke out for the non-condemnation of the suspect. When, however, no proceedings for the taking of evidence can be conducted, a suspect can still be punished, for example with a penalty that lies with the discretion of the judge and possibly can still contain the death penalty if the judge assumes that he is dealing with particularly severe guilt.

Confessions can be retracted up to the time that the punishment is carried out or can be thrown out by a judge for lack of credibility. Moreover, capital offenses are under exceedingly short statutes of limitation. A circumstantial legal case (for instance, in the case of the pregnancy of an unmarried woman) are possible in isolated cases.[46] However, they do not correspond to the classical proceedings for the taking of evidence or conviction on the basis of eyewitness reports.[47]

All of this reduces hearings of capital offenses in court, as does the fact that most capital offenses – in particular cases of adultery and fornication – can rarely be brought before court. Rather, the woman in particular is more likely punished with lashes, locked up, or killed by her own family. If a capital offense is nevertheless brought before court, a representative case is made or a power struggle is staged, in which a member of an uninfluential minority that has no societal protective mechanisms at his disposal is designated as a victim for a politically ambitious group. It is for this reason

---

[45] Silvia Tellenbach. *Strafgesetze der Islamischen Republik Iran* (Berlin, 1996), p. 47.

[46] Comp. the list of methods of providing evidence in criminal law trials in Mohamed S. El-Awa. *Punishment in Islamic Law: A Comparative Study* (American Trust Publications: Indianapolis, 1993), S. 124ff.

[47] Iran's criminal code does not consider an extramarital pregnancy to be sufficient evidence of illicit sexual activity, but rather incorporates the possibility of rape: Silvia Tellenbach, *Strafgesetze der Islamischen Republik Iran* (Walter de Gruyter: Berlin, 1996), p. 14.

one assumes that in the case of the Egyptian publicist Farag Fouda, who was murdered in 1993 by extremists, *"the call for the Sharia is not so much a question of belief but rather an embellished religio-political power struggle for domination."*[48]

Overall Sharia law is extremely seldom applied in criminal law, although at the same time, as far as its theoretical claims are concerned, it is nowhere officially negated or relativized. In most cases it is de facto set aside in that it, for example, is argued that it can only be applied in a truly Islamic country and not in a country that does not fulfill these conditions.

What are the offenses that call for retaliation?

The second category of wrongdoings is offenses with retaliation against the body and the life of a person, such as murder or manslaughter. According to the Sharia, murder and manslaughter do not infringe upon divine law but rather only upon human law, while adultery and the consumption of alcohol fall into the category of capital offenses that infringe upon God's law.[49]

Offenses calling for retaliation allow for the penalty of inflicting the same injury or taking the life of the murderer or the individual who committed manslaughter under the supervision of a judge who – if the eligible individual waives the right – can take payment in blood money instead. In addition, there is a religious work of penance. This could be, for example, additional fasting (Sura 2:178-179). In a legal sense only an individual of majority age, who is in complete control of his mental faculties, is guilty.

Insofar as a person is killed in a premeditated manner, the family of the person killed can call for the killing of the guilty individual. However, only the nearest male relative is allowed to make this request and no other person. Along with this there is the principle of equity: a woman for a woman, a slave for a slave. "O you who believe! retaliation is prescribed for you in the matter of the slain, the free for the free, and the slave for the slave, and the female for the female ..." (Sura 2:178). If this equity cannot be produced, then no retaliation may be exercised.

The family of a victim can waive the killing of the guilty individual and instead accept the payment of blood money (Arabic *diya*). In Iran the blood money for a Muslim man is currently 100 flawless camels, 200 head of

---

[48] Ermute Heller; Hassouna Mosbahi. *Islam, Demokratie, Moderne. Aktuelle Antworten arabischer Denker.* (C. H. Beck: München, 1998), p. 24.

[49] Konrad Dilger; „Tendenzen der Rechtsentwicklung" in Werner Ende, Udo Steinbach, *Der Islam in der Gegenwart (*München, 1996/4), p. 206.

The Main Contents of the Sharia 41

cattle or 1,000 muttons, 200 Yemeni garments and 1,000 Dinari or 10,000 silver Dirham.[50] As a rule, the amount for a woman amounts to one-half, and likewise for a non-Muslim, also according to the Iranian criminal code the amount is less.

If a victim only receives an injury, the culprit can theoretically be given the same injury. However, the injury is to be given by the victim himself. If the victim waives the right to vengeance, compensation can be paid in this case as well.

Retaliation may only seldom be applied, but its 'informal' expression as blood vengeance, without the involvement of a judge or court, is frequently found in countries shaped by Islam.

What are discretionary offenses?

All other cases, which belong neither to the categories of capital offenses and offenses calling for retaliation, are, with respect to their punishment, left to the discretion of the judge. For example, rioting, giving false witness, libel, bribery, forgery, embezzlement, traffic violations, fraud, extortion, kidnapping, among others, as well as capital offenses which, for instance, cannot be punished as capital offenses for the lack of evidence, also all belong to this category.

The judge can impose punishments such as long jail sentences (limited or open-ended imprisonment), banishment, lashings (the opinions of Muslim theologians varies from 20 to 99 lashings[51]), or fines. A judge can remove an offender from his post or seize his possessions. However, a simple warning or reproach can count as discretionary punishment. The judge can publicly denounce the individual and issue a warning that the person is untrustworthy.[52] In difficult cases coming under the category of discretionary offenses, the judge can even impose the death penalty. This can occur, according to a broadly held notion that above all has to do with repeat offenders without the prospect for a mending of ways: homosexuals, those who declare heresies or split Islamic society, murderers (insofar as their actions cannot be avenged via retaliation), drug dealers, or spies. However, the right to impose the death penalty is a disputed issue among legal scholars: Some theologians are of the opinion that a discretionary penalty may

---

[50] Silvia Tellenbach, *Strafgesetze der Islamischen Republik Iran* (Berlin 1996), pp. 96-97.

[51] Mohammed S. El-Awa, *Punishment in Islamic Law: A Comparative Study* (Indiana/USA, 1993), p. 107.

[52] Ibid., pp. 102-103.

never reach the extent of capital punishment. The spectrum of statutory offenses that fall into the discretionary realm of a judge is immense.

Does the Sharia live up to its claims?

If one truly judges according to the Sharia, one sees that it cannot be reconciled with constitutional structures, because of the lack of clear predictability of the level of punishment. Also, due to the option of unlimited imprisonment, there is no predictability of when punishment ends. Apart from that, stonings, or for that matter lashings, are cruel methods of punishment and execution. In the case of amputations no rehabilitation is possible, because an amputee is thereby stigmatized forever and additionally such an individual is permanently dependent on society for care. A reprieve is no longer possible for the individual. Retaliation is also irreconcilable with Western notions of justice, as it is a type of private revenge, which can evoke an escalation of vengeance and then more vengeance. Furthermore, the criminal code discriminates against women and non-Muslims and denies converts the right to life.

Islamic criminal law is distinguished by several features: On the one hand there are harshly stiff penalties for capital offenses, such as lashings, amputation, stoning, and crucifixion. At the same time, demanding evidential requirements are also features of the Sharia. Such demanding rules of evidence make a court proceeding for capital punishment extremely difficult to conduct, and in the case of adultery or fornication, which requires four male eyewitnesses, it is as much as impossible. These circumstances, and the Near Eastern-Muslim notion of honor and shame, which expose the woman as the carrier of honor to severe sanctions, make private revenge for an alleged or actual offense more probable. This is due to the fact that there is a partial notion in society that punishment inflicted by the family is not an additional injustice but is rather anticipatory of judicial justice.

Again and again Muslim legal practitioners have emphasized that the Sharia may only be applied if several basic condition are met, such as, for example, mental soundness, knowledge of the legal framework indicated by the age of puberty as well as free will (the absence of coercion, self-defense, or intoxicants and controlled substances) when a criminal offense is committed.[53] While several legal scholars, for instance al-Juwaini (d. 1085), advocate that an individual who was drunk cannot be fully criminal-

---

[53] See the list of legal preliminaries, for instance, in: Ahmad Hasan, *Principles of Islamic Jurisprudence*, vol. 1. (Islamic Research Institute, Publication No. 89, International Islamic University: Islamabad, 1993), p. 294ff.

ly liable,[54] the Iranian criminal code emphasizes that the punishment cannot be reduced if the offender imbibed alcoholic beverages for the purpose of committing the offense.[55] Forgetfulness, periodically dwindling consciousness, or the mistaken assumption of other facts and circumstances (for instance the assumption of entering into a legal marriage with a certain woman) are found in classical legal literature to be reasons for reducing or suspending punishment that the Sharia would impose. For this reason, precisely, capital offenses can only be committed with premeditation.

Since only an adult male Muslim is considered to have legal capacity and to be responsible for his actions, in the legal literature women are partially viewed as limited in their responsibility for their actions, and their punishment in the case of capital offenses can be diminished (according to the opinion of some legal schools, the threat of corporal punishment and imprisonment, and not the death penalty, should apply to female apostasy).

Taking refuge through assuming inverted conditions, that is, for instance, the contention that the accused was not in full possession of his rational faculties at the time of the crime (as was, for example, the case with Abdurrahman, a convert to Christianity in Afghanistan in 2006 who was condemned to death[56]) has often prevented the actual application of the stiffest sentence. Adel Theodor Khoury correctly emphasizes that also in the case where the death penalty has not been applied in the specific situation of a renunciation of Islam (only in the most rare cases may a case of apostasy be brought before a court), "*as the legal sanction for apostasy the death penalty ... [nevertheless retains] its validity.*"[57] At least as far as its claim is concerned, up until now one cannot speak of any actual reform or relativizing.

According to the opinion of Muslim apologists, Islamic criminal law finds its legitimacy, on the one hand, from the fact that it was given by God himself and for that reason stands above all human legislation. This basic difference between 'divine inspiration,' which "*reflects the perfection, glory and light of the omnipresence of God,*" and the 'human crea-

---

[54] According to Tilman Nagel, *Das islamische Recht: Eine Einführung* (WVA-Verlag Skulima: Westhofen, 2001), p. 34.

[55] Silvia Tellenbach. *Strafgesetze der Islamischen Republik Iran* (Walter de Gruyter: Berlin, 1996), p. 10.

[56] Comp. the summary report. http://de.wikipedia.org/wiki/Abdul_Rahman_(Konvertit) (31.3.2007).

[57] Adel Theodor Khoury, *Der Koran, Arabisch-Deutsch* (Gütersloher Verlagshaus Gerd Mohn: Gütersloh, 1991), vol. 2, p. 95.

tion' of a law is always highlighted.[58] It is said to create a fairer society in that it *"protects life, physical integrity, and honor and has the general character of ensuring freedom."*[59] Also in this vein are Muslim theologians' and legal practitioners' repeated calls for public enforcement of punishment as a manner of deterrence. *"Humiliation of the guilty person and instruction of the public are the intentions of punishment."*[60]

In addition, Islamic criminal law is said to be more appropriate than the criminal law of Western countries with their concentration on prisons (and to a lesser degree fines), since Islamic law is more effective in deterring offenses. Besides, an offender does not become a burden to society by being sentenced to a long period of imprisonment.[61] In fact, however, jail sentences in Islamic countries can be very long and can be extended indefinitely.

The fight for the implementation of the Sharia

If someone had assumed thirty or forty years ago that the authority of the Sharia would diminish in the course of globalization, and that the Islamic world would be taken in by the advanced secularization of the West, by the 1970s at the latest it would have become clear that the opposite development, that is to say a return and reorientation towards Islamic law, had started. However, Islamification by creating a carefully considered set of detailed laws – the basis of which is solely the Sharia – and the production of a complete and practical legal codex, has been shown to be extremely difficult. Disappointed by Western politics and the pursuit of self-serving interests, confronted by various internal problems such as high unemployment, overpopulation, educational plight, a largely absent infrastructure, and underdevelopment, the Islamic world sought a new direction in the return to Islam. As a part of this, Islamists called for the complete introduction of Islam into society and the return of 'the golden age of Islam' from the time of Mohammed and the first four caliphs in an effort to give back to the Islamic world the strength and supremacy of past centuries.

---

[58] Also, for example, Abdul Qader 'Oud Shaheed, *Criminal Law of Islam* 2 vols., (International Islamic Publishers: New Delhi, 1991), here vol. 1, pp. 15-16.

[59] Lorenz Müller, *Islam und Menschenrechte: Sunnitische Muslime zwischen Islamismus, Säkularismus und Modernismus* (Deutsches Orient-Institut: Hamburg, 1996), p. 182.

[60] Mohammad Iqbal Siddiqi, *The Penal Law of Islam* (International Islamic Publishers: New Delhi, 1994), p. 9.

[61] So lectures Nagaty Sanad, *The Theory of Crime and Criminal Responsibility in Islamic Law: Shari'a* (Chicago, Illinois, USA, 1991), pp. 56-57.

However, numerous Muslim theologians and legal theorists have already acknowledged the serious problems in this area. They recognize that the introduction of Islamic criminal law into a society that is determined by many non-Islamic principles would be senseless. "The ideal Islamic society" that corresponds to the original Islamic community would have to be first established before Islamic criminal law could truly come to be applied.[62] Looked at realistically, this is a stipulation that cannot be fulfilled.

Wherever the Sharia has already been put partially into practice, it has not yet fulfilled its promise to bring dignity, freedom, and justice to people. Minorities and women are those who suffer most on the way to the alleged complete Islamization of society. On the one hand, a particular set of problems lie in the unquestioned exemplary character of Mohammed and all of his actions. On the other hand, there is the failure to critically evaluate and historically relativize the classical Islamic legal system, which is related to the largely missing free intra-Muslim discourse regarding the reevaluation and repositioning of the Sharia in modern times.

---

[62] This is emphasized, for instance, by the former professor for Islamic law at the University of Riyadh and legal adviser of the educational authorities of the Gulf States, Mohamed S. El-Awa. *Punishment in Islamic Law: A Comparative Study* (American Trust Publications: Indianapolis, 1993), p. 138.

The Sharia in Europe?

The migration of Muslims to Germany

Although this factor was pushed to the side for decades, Germany's multi-religious and multi-cultural society has been a reality for a long time. Who would have thought, after the end of World War II and in the hour of the birth of a German democracy, to give the founding fathers of the Federal Republic cause for concern in the formulation of the German Constitution due to the fact that on the eve of the new millennium over 3 million Muslims would live in Germany and that a politically organized and networked Islam would insistently call for equal treatment alongside Christian churches? Surely no one.

The religious and cultural face of the Federal Republic has undergone sustained change over the past 60 years. Today Islam, with its variety of Islamic groupings and estimated 3.2 million people adhering to the Muslim faith,[63] has become an irreversible part of German society. And the numbers continue to rise. At the same time, the German population has declined since 2003. Germany formerly had 82.5 million people, but the population will shrink to between 69 and 74 million from 2005 to 2050. In contrast to other assumptions, the birth rate of migrants, which is still 30 percent higher than that of Germans, is also continually falling such that the population total will not remain stable.[64]

The history of Islam in German began in 1961, when the first contracts were concluded to recruit Muslim workers from Turkey. Largely untrained workers – even in part illiterate – came as *Gastarbeiter* (guest workers) from Anatolia to Germany. Many men came alone and initially left their families in Turkey. These Turkish *Gastarbeiter* primarily found work in underground mining, in the steel and construction industries, and in auto plants in order to promote the colossal growth in post-war Germany. There was full employment at the time, and no additional work force reserves could be mustered from within the borders of Europe. From the German as well as the Turkish side it was assumed that the time Turkish workers would spend in Germany would be a matter of several years.

---

[63] Since no official membership exists within Islamic religious communities, membership statistics regarding Islam cannot be compiled.

[64] Source: Federal Statistical Office, Wiesbaden: http://www.distatis.de/presse/deutsch/pk/2006/bevoelkerungsprojektion2050i.pdf, pp. 5, 30 (November 15, 2006).

In 1973, at the time of the first economic crisis, the employment situation in Germany had changed. A halt to the recruiting was decreed, but it remained possible for families to be reunited. At that time 910,500 Turks lived in the Federal Republic of Germany.[65] Due to the somewhat unsure political situation in Turkey and the fact that the economic outlook was not particularly promising, many Turks indefinitely delayed their plans to return and many families remained. Their children represented the second generation of Muslims in Germany.

With a higher birth rate in comparison to the German population, and through refugees and immigrants from various Islamic countries (above all from Bosnia-Herzegovina, Iran, Afghanistan, Pakistan and several Arab countries such as Iraq, Lebanon, Syria, Tunisia, and Morocco[66]), who had fled from wars and crises, as well as by those seeking asylum and economic migrants, the number of Muslims in Germany has grown to what is currently an estimated 3.2 million people.[67] One can add to this number an estimated 500,000 to two million people illegally in Germany, a part of which is Muslim.[68] There are already grandchildren of *Gastarbeiter* (guest workers) in Germany, that is to say, the third generation of migrant workers, among them around 800,000 Muslim children and youth. Up until at least 1980, the assumption of politicians as well as of the general public was that Muslim *Gastarbeiter* would soon return to Turkey. Even if this was the case for many families over the decades, there was never the ex-

---

[65] This number is mentioned by Lachmann, Günther, *Tödliche Toleranz: Die Muslime und unsere offene Gesellschaft* (München 2005/2), p. 23.

[66] Comp. the numbers from the Federal Statistical Office, Wiesbaden: Ausländerzentralregister, extract dated December 31, 2005 (information per email on November 15, 2006).

[67] Religious affiliation is not recorded in the central registry of aliens (*Ausländerzentralregister*). Additionally, a portion of the Muslim population has received German citizenship. The total Muslim population can be indirectly deduced from the number of foreign persons residing in Germany (at the end of 2003 approximately 2.6 million), from the number of naturalized citizens from countries with predominantly Muslim religious affiliation, the number of Muslim children born in Germany who have received German citizenship at birth, and a number extrapolated from the 50,000 German converts at the time of the 1987 census: Federal Statistical Office, Wiesbaden (information per email on November 15, 2006). Regarding the phenomenon of conversion to Islam in Western societies compare the foundational study by Monika Wohlrab-Sahr, *Konversion zum Islam in Deutschland und den USA* (Frankfurt, 1999).

[68] In the 1990s the estimates reached 1 million people: Bommes, Michael; Schiffauer, Werner (eds.). *Migrationsreport 2006. Fakten, Analysen, Perspektiven* (Frankfurt, 2006), p. 44.

pected wave of people returning home. An unfortunate result was that there were only a few consequences with respect to concrete political action that addressed the integration of those who would live permanently in Germany.

Dealing with Islam – facing reality or living in denial?

With the influx of families, in particular in the 1970s and 1980s, came the first visible indications of Muslim life in Germany: Turkish stores opened, religious festivals were celebrated in city areas strongly influenced by Turkish inhabitants, traditions (mostly rural) were above all passed on by women to following generations, culture centers and more mosques (not only in rear courtyards and factory buildings) were opened, the amplified calls to prayer or the height of minarets at times became the subject of lawsuits, young girls were often married off in Turkey or a rural bride brought to Germany. All of this, as well as the increasing social tension associated with the large number of immigrants and the increasing worry about keeping one's own job, left the indigenous population with a feeling of being threatened, a feeling of foreign infiltration, and a feeling of disdain for the Turkish population. In the 1990s this culminated in several violent and appalling outrages against Turkish migrants.

During the first decades of migration one can agree with Günther Lachmann. He has stated the following: *"In the late 70s and early 80s most Germans refused to see immigrants as a permanent and immovable component of society."*[69]

In the 1980s it was still more or less assumed that the integration of those who would stay would almost take place on its own and not require any particular attention. As late as the 1990s, people in positions of responsibility held to the thesis that by the second or third generation, the religio-cultural values of immigrants from Muslim culture would have become so subordinated to secular, pluralistic, and postmodern society that their particular ancestry would be of no consequence. It would no longer even be recognizable. This is now seen to have been a misconception that is today all too evident. The second and at latest the third generation would speak German without error and of course proficiently. Separate remedial language instruction would not be required – and that, too, was a misconception. And finally, it was more or less officially presumed that as a religion, Islam and the cultural values that were founded upon it would not play an appreciable role. The thought was that Islam would soon be 'enlightened'

---

[69] Lachmann, Günther, *Tödliche Toleranz*: *Die Muslime und unsere offene Gesellschaft* (München 2005/2), p. 49.

and take on a marginal existence in the private sphere of believers as Christianity had done in Western society. However, just the opposite has occurred.

In the first twenty or thirty years it was not recognized that the second and third generations of migrant workers would need programs to assist them. On the other side, and in the shadows of mosques, political networks arose which aggressively questioned the values and foundations of Western society. These political networks often openly rejected the values and foundations of Western society and used their influence to warn Muslim believers about the "Godless West" and to make a call to distance oneself from 'unbelievers.' As a result of rapidly increasing unemployment in the construction industry, technological advances and computerization, and layoffs of unqualified labor that came as a result, not to mention closings in fields of work inherently manned by migrants, such as blast furnaces and strip mining, all too many families became dependent upon state aid. This negative development was conditioned by the prevailingly weak educational background of the immigrants.

Aside from immigrants, it is thought that about 10,000 to 12,000 Germans have converted to Islam (some Muslim organizations report larger numbers), whereby it can be assumed that we are primarily talking about women in bi-religious marriages. However, in addition, there are people in Germany who today convert to Islam due to personal convictions. In the meantime, nearly 1 million people with Turkish ancestry possess a German passport.

The history of Islam in Germany, then, already comprises a time period of nearly fifty years, the smallest portion of which has been consciously molded and which, given the growing number of immigrants, has long not been recognized for its importance with respect to political and societal challenges.

How Islam is organized in Germany

German Islam is characterized by its Turkish expression. Approximately 2.6 million people in Germany have Turkish ancestry. In addition, there are several hundred thousand Arabs from various countries and more than 100,000 Iranians. This produces a heterogeneous picture. However, Islam associated with Turkish backgrounds is neither ethnically nor religiously homogeneous. This means that out of those people in Germany who have Turkish passports, there is a large Kurdish minority. At the same time not all people from Turkey belong to Sunni Islam, which is the major Islamic denomination. There are around 350,000 to 400,000 Alevi Muslims in

Germany, who indeed are predominantly of Turkish ancestry but who, in their religious practice, differ significantly from Turkish Sunnis.

Turkish Islam is basically characterized by laicism. Kemal Ataturk, the 'father of Turkey,' accomplished the official separation of state and religion with the removal of the Ottoman Empire and the founding of the Turkish Republic in 1923/1924. He also placed the army as a guard over this state-prescribed laicism. Representatives of the apolitical Islam of the Turkish state are called the Turkish-Islamic Union for Religious Affairs (in German: *Türkisch-Islamische Union der Anstalt für Religion e. V.: DİTİB*), who send most of the imams (prayer leaders in the mosques) to Germany. On Fridays DİTİB mosques read out predefined sermons from Ankara and are generally considered to be representatives of a moderate, apolitical Islam which is open to dialog. However, as a rule DİTİB imams are replaced every two to four years. Due to their generally meager German language skills, their sphere of influence is primarily limited to their own Turkish community.

Nevertheless, there are also political groups within Turkish Islam. The largest group considered to be Islamic extremist by the Federal Office for the Protection of the Constitution, Milli Görüs, has just under 30,000 members. Islamic groups frequently call upon their members to separate themselves from German society. In particular cities this withdrawal from German society and ghettoization can now be observed more strongly than in the past. Since over the past forty years in Germany – and this unfortunately also applies in large part to churches and religious communities – people have neglected to approach Muslims, this withdrawal by the Muslim community and current terrorist attacks have heightened the resistance and fear many people experience.

Other Muslim organizations in Germany are the Central Council of Muslims in Germany, with perhaps 12,000 to 15,000 members, the Islamic Council (in German: *Islamrat*), with possibly 150,000 members, and the Association of Muslim Cultural Centers (in German: *Verband der Islamischen Kulturzentren*), which has largely withdrawn from any public relations efforts. In March 2007 these three associations, together with the DİTİB, founded the Coordinating Council of Muslims (in German: *Koordinierungsrat der Muslime in Deutschland: KRM*) as the official contact for the state and church, since in principle in Islamic religious communities there is no membership and no church structure. A difficulty exists, however, in the fact that only around 8 to 10 percent of all Muslims in Germany have organized themselves. This means that the Coordinating Council of Muslims represents an absolute minority.

The current Sharia discussion in Europe

Given neglected integration and the establishment of political organizations within the Muslim community, the topic of the 'Sharia in Germany' has become an issue which German society and politics can no longer ignore. With that said, the Islamic community in Germany is not an isolated entity. Rather, it is always to be considered with reference to theological and political developments in people's countries of origin. This is due to the fact that, via Islamic political groups in Germany, attempts are made in the countries of origin to exert influence on the Muslim community in Europe.

If the 'Sharia in Germany' topic seemed to be far-fetched or even completely absurd a few years ago, today it is intensively discussed and rightly so. Where the 'Sharia in Germany' topic is discussed, it is, however, rarely the criminal portion of the Sharia which is meant. This means that the debate is not intended to be about introducing amputations, whippings, and stonings. Instead, it above all has to do with the area of marital and family law.

On the one hand, it is inappropriate within the Sharia discussion to warn of an imminent introduction of the Sharia as if it is a real possibility that could replace the Constitution in Germany tomorrow. Muslims will certainly not represent the majority of the population in Germany in the near future in spite of the dropping number of ancestral Germans and the higher birth rate among Muslim immigrants. However, the pressure from migration arising from economic refugees, the politically persecuted, and immigrants from countries shaped by Islam who come to Germany due to marriage, will probably continue to be strong.

On the other hand, it should not be overlooked that Islamic groups and umbrella organizations which are political in nature are trying to prepare the soil for the presence of the Sharia. Initially this happens by familiarizing the public with Islamic legal theory and the foundations of Islamic theology and social order and by calling for respect for Islam and its social as well as legal components. In light of current events, a number of activists in Muslim organizations maintain that they are not adequately recognized as Muslims in German society, that they do not receive sufficient state support with building plans or with educational initiatives, and that legally they are not placed on an equal footing with Christian churches. This means that there is a limitation on religious freedom, indeed even discrimination. It is not seldom that in this connection charges of racism and Islamophobia are made. And under the allegation of supposed discrimination, increased special rights are called for by the Muslim minority with the assertion that certain particularities are prescribed as obligatory for Muslims on the basis of their belief, i.e., that these items are part of the religious commands coming from the Sharia. The state here in Germany would have to ensure that Muslims can, for example, buy ritually slaughtered meat (in Arabic: halal) everywhere and for that reason legally regulate unanesthetized religious slaughter.

Indeed, at the same time it is emphasized that there is in no way a desire to introduce the Sharia in Germany in its fullness (also admittedly a utopian demand at this time), since a complete implementation of the Sharia would only be thinkable in a 'truly' Islamic State, and Germany is not representative of such a state. But can that actually be a source of calm? The claim that the Sharia is a system of regulations for all areas of life and a superior legal system which promotes peace for all people is also something that cannot essentially be abandoned by Muslims who hold fast to the foundations of their faith in the diaspora. This is the case, even if here in our country Sharia criminal law and procedures have no validity whatsoever – as is also the case in most Islamic countries. Whoever holds to the duty of praying five times daily, performs ritual washings, follows dress and dietary laws, holds the month of fasting, and holds to the duty to participate in pilgrimage for reasons of faith can only with difficulty find justification for distancing himself from the legal components of that same set of laws. That would only be possible if the individual performed a historical-critical division into those regulations which are still valid and those Sharia regulations which are no longer practicable in modernity. Such a historical-critical evaluation or even an essential distancing from the validity of the Sharia for modern times is currently, at most, a matter of private conviction on the part of individuals, e.g., of intellectuals, reformers, or women's rights and human rights activists. However, this has not achieved general validity due to the shortcoming that Islam and its history have not undergone an enlightened, historical-critical evaluation.

Therefore, the discussion does not run along lines between Muslim groups who principally advocate the claim for the Sharia and those who basically reject it. This is due to the fact that the theoretical demands of the Sharia indeed stand largely unchallenged in the numerically vastly dominant realm of conservative theological thought. As a general rule, this claim is also theoretically shared by those who do not socially and politically advocate moving closer to this goal in Europe. One speaks at this point of the apolitical majority of Muslims in Germany, who, for want of official mouthpieces and platforms for their concerns, often make up a silent majority: For the most part, they do not explicitly act against those who speak for politically engaged Muslim organizations and who would like to take the majority captive to their political agenda. For that reason, it is often difficult for the observer to gauge which portion of Muslims in Germany would, for example, actively advocate the absolute equality of women (including entirely free choice with respect to profession and choice of partner and dispensing with the Sharia-based principle of obedience and the marital right of the husband to chastise the wife). In so doing, an individual would esteem the constitution and the social norms of Germany higher than the religiously defined Sharia norms and homelike traditions denying women certain rights and, with that said, place them at a legal disadvantage.

Such a theological and legal discussion regarding the commitments to and limits of Sharia law in the diaspora is hardly conducted within the Muslim community – outside of the private sphere. The discussion is primarily decided in practice: Muslims in the second or third generation increasingly orient themselves more or – in particular during their youth – less strongly towards the social traditions or legally prescribed Sharia norms, without opposing the claims of the Sharia in critical, public discourse. This circumstance is used by politically active Muslim groups for the purpose of claiming legal space for the entire Muslim community in certain questions and stigmatizing its rejection as discrimination and as placing individuals at a disadvantage.

As a rule, these demands involve one-sided and very conservatively interpreted rules of behavior, which are viewed as essentially incompatible with Western lifestyles, such as swimming lessons for girls. If one can understand that co-educational swimming lessons would be unthinkable in a conservative Islamic household in the country of origin, this discussion then becomes a political issue. This is particularly the case if certain groups representatively interpret participation in swim lessons for all Muslims as a 'betrayal of the faith' and offer all sorts of legal assistance – such as prepackaged forms or legal advice – in order to induce as many families as possible to withdraw their daughters from swim lessons.

A further strategy involves attempts to bring cases before the Federal Constitutional Court and the Federal Administrative Court as a use of legal means to bring change to the existing legal system in the name of religious freedom, or at least to familiarize the public with the fact that there are a number of areas where Muslims claim alternative legal norms for themselves. Politics in the name of Islam, or more specifically Islamist efforts, do not directly have anything to do with violence in such cases; that is the realm of extremism which also advocates the use of violence in the name of Islam. Islamism, however, which attests to no less resolve, conducts politics in democracies by exploiting feasible paths in the name of a minority.

- Politics in the name of Islam is, for example, also conducted at that point where the battle for permission to carry out unanesthetized religious slaughter of sacrificial animals for Islamic holidays occurs: After all German animal protection advocates' efforts were in vain with respect to persuading acceptance of completely bleeding animals anesthetized by electroshock, exceptions were allowed under animal protection law.

- It is not only where Muslim children are withdrawn from swim lessons that it is a question of politics. Rather, it has to do with withdrawal from the entire physical education program, and indeed in part even withdrawal from biology, music, or art instruction. Most frequently, however, it has to do with withdrawal from school trips.

- Included in political lobbying efforts is also the battle regarding the headscarf for permanent teachers, whereby political umbrella organizations very energetically supported the first claimant who pursued the issue in the court system.

- Politics in the name of Islam also plays a role when it is a question of the construction of prestigious, oversized mosques, higher minarets, and calls to prayer employing loudspeakers. It also has to do with politics when it comes to attempts at influencing the manner of reporting done by the media and to bringing charges of racism, Islamophobia, and xenophobia in the face of what is undesired (in particular critical reports). This also includes the charge repeatedly brought forth in various contexts that the position and treatment of Muslims in Europe is to be compared with that of the Jews at the time of National Socialism. This charge was already brought forth decades ago, for example, when calls were made to introduce Islamic religious instruction nationwide. It surfaced most recently during the so-called 'cartoon controversy' in 2006. Faruk Sen, the prior head of the Center for Turkish Studies in Essen, Germany, who has lived in Germany for decades, made statements in May 2008 in a Turkish newspaper that Muslims, with respect to their discrimination and exclusion from society, are the 'new Jews of Europe.'[70] With regard to the German past, this is truly an egregious

---

[70] Comp. for instance the report: http://www.faz.net/s/RubDDBDABB9457A437BA A85A49C26FB23A0/Doc~EA45EC73E13834109845B5EEDC43FF3DE~ATpl~ Ecommon~Scontent.html (February 14, 2009).

charge which discredits itself both through the incomparability of the two eras and the different social-political circumstances.

It can be assumed that the comparison to the Nazi regime and its circumstances, in the face of what can be a rather fierce exchange of blows in the media surrounding partially failed integration, is being used with the goal of capitalizing on historical feelings of guilt in the German population.

In this connection, there is also the mechanism which, on various occasions, disputes what has been exposed in the press or by authors of books with regard to problematic developments within the Muslim community or in Islamic tradition. In an offended and angry tone, it can also ascribe maliciousness, Islamophobia, and prejudice-laden attitudes to analysts, promptly blaming the majority German society and its alleged hostility to Islam.

- Something similar happened in 2006, for example, upon the occasion of the helping hand given by Evangelical Church in Germany (EKD) in the form of the published work *Clarity and Good Neighborly Relations Christians and Muslims in Germany*.[71] Fierce charges were made with respect to the text by representatives of Muslim umbrella organizations without having been able to use Islamic sources to demonstrate errors in the work, i.e., without using sources of Islamic theology or tradition.

- A similar thing happened in November 2006, when, due to concerns about attacks, the opera *Idomeneo* was canceled in the face of subtle threats: What emerges is a climate of continual calculating and worry about what reactions might come from the Muslim side in the face of art or critique. That was at a time – for instance during the 2006 'cartoon controversy' – when owing to the rioting, killing, and extensive destruction at that time the climate suddenly changed to one of fear and intimidation. Such incidents continue to have an effect and impressively warn everyone against getting too close to Islam and its adherents in any way. All of that illustrates efforts at, first of all, creating an awareness that Islam is a social as well as politically influential force in Germany that is not to be neglected. Furthermore, this has also developed similarly throughout Europe and demonstrates a desire to be treated as an equal partner by the church and the political system.

---

[71] *Clarity and Good Neighborly Relations Christians and Muslims in Germany*. A helping hand from the Council of the Evangelical Church in Germany (EKD). EKD Texte 86, Hannover 2006 (http://www.ekd.de/english/download/EKD-Text-86-englisch-revised.pdf).

What is interesting in this connection is the introduction of so-called Sharia legal courts in a number of European countries. In Great Britain, there are Sharia courts which are operating with state approval in order to regulate civil justice issues such as divorce, but they also address domestic violence or disputes regarding financial matters within the Muslim community:[72] The introduction of Sharia jurisdiction was made possible by a law having to do with courts of arbitration going back to 1996. At that time Sharia courts were labeled mediation courts. According to the law, the decisions of such courts are binding if the parties acknowledge the court for their case. Sheikh Faiz-ul-Aqtab Siddiqi, who runs the new Sharia courts, declared that it was a question of exploiting a loophole in order to introduce the judgments of Sharia courts, which are courts of arbitration, into the British legal system. As a matter of fact, an extra form of administering justice is not only available to Muslims. For more than 100 years, Jewish Beth Din courts have tried civil cases.[73] Canada can also be mentioned as taking a particularly prominent position in connection with Sharia courts: In that country, the Muslim women's rights movement has battled for the abolishment of these instances of religious jurisdiction in the past few years.

By reason of such developments alone, above all in neighboring European countries, a similar discussion can also not be avoided here at home, especially in certain cases when Sharia law has already here applied here in Germany. This has been the case, for example, with court decisions in family law where they have been made in terms of the countries of origin (influenced by Islam) for foreign married couples and the legislation there. This have been done to the extent that there nas not been a contradiction of the fundamental rights found within Germany's legal system.

It is more a matter of Sharia law 'on the street level' when certain Muslim and often nationally uniform groups have attempted to implement a part of Sharia law in particular city districts with a high Muslim share of the population – above all with respect to 'correct' dress for women and their corresponding behavior.

When it comes to the question of the demand to introduce the Sharia in Germany and the question of how large the share of the Muslim population is in Germany which recognizes its own frame of reference within Islamic law, the study published by the Federal Ministry of the Interior in 2007

---

[72] See the report at http://www.timesonline.co.uk/tol/news/uk/crime/article4749183.ece (February 14, 2.2009).

[73] http://www.timesonline.co.uk/tol/news/uk/crime/article4749183.ece (February 14, 2.2009).

entitled *Muslims in Germany* is of great interest.[74] Over the course of three years, colleagues of the Hamburg criminologists Karin Brettfled and Peter Wetzels made inquiries into the attitudes of Muslims in Germany and on the topics of integration and democracy, rule of law, and politically-religiously motivated violence.

An initial survey was directed at a non-specified group of the Muslim residential population, which through a standardized telephone survey reached about 1,000 people. The results of these interviews were contrasted with the answers of three particular groups: 500 pupils in the 9th and 10th grades between the ages of 14 and 18, 150 Muslim students, and 60 members, or more specifically, activists in Islamic associations, organizations, and mosques. Therefore, overall there were answers from over 1,700 Muslims taken into account in the analysis. The educational level of those participating ranged from Muslims in non-college preparatory high school to the university level, and the age range covered the entire spectrum beginning at 14 years of age. The geographical area of the research included the cities of Hamburg, Berlin, Cologne, and Augsburg. The majority of those questioned were of Turkish descent, which also corresponds to the national distribution within the Muslim community in Germany.

An important if not surprising result when viewed against the backdrop of earlier studies was that the majority of Muslims in Germany are closely tied to their religion in theory and in practice. The number of those individuals who consider themselves to be religious or very religious has again risen over the past years. Over 85% of the Muslims in Germany label themselves as 'devout' or 'very devout.' The number of individuals who go to a mosque at least once per week rose from 30.7% to 41.6% between 2000 and 2005. Of those participating, 89% either 'completely' agree or 'rather' agree with the statement, that the Koran is the revelation of God. A directly political-fundamentalist tendency, however, can only be ascribed to a minority among this religious majority.

It is not only mosque attendance which has increased. Rather, it is also the number of individuals advocating the wearing of headscarves by women: In 2005, 46.6% agreed that women should wear a headscarf in public, whereas only 27.2% answered in the affirmative in 2000. Also, among younger Muslims in Germany, the number of individuals who have visited a Koran school is notably higher than among older individuals. Interestingly, the highest per-

---

[74] *Muslims in Germany*. A study by the Federal Ministry of the Interior on Integration, Barriers to Integration, Religion and Attitudes Toward Democracy, the Constitutional State, and Politically and Religiously Motivated Violence. Results of Surveys Within the Framework of a Multicentric Study in Urban Environments, by Kathrin Brettfeld and Peter Wetzels, 509 pp., Hamburg, 2007.

centage is among those born in Germany (60.2%). The longer the period of attendance at a Koran school, the stronger a fundamental religious orientation is expressed, and against the background of results of earlier studies about the integration-inhibiting role of Koran schools, this is likewise not surprising.[75]

The study emphatically emphasizes, and rightly so, that an orthodox, traditional, or fundamental orientation towards religion should not prematurely be equated with readiness to use violence and extremism. In no way does Islam teach terrorism as a goal of faith, and whoever prays five times daily is for that reason not an extremist and a perpetrator of violence. In order to slide from religiously (strict) belief into extremism, additional fostering moments are required. The study recognizes three significant factors on the path to radicalization:

For the first, essentially adaptable group, it is above all the personal experiences of rejection by the majority society which lead these people to distance themselves from Western society. At the same time, this group has few chances for social participation on the basis of their low level of education. For the second group, it is less the experience of personal exclusion and more the representative feeling that, as a Muslim, one is the victim of global oppression. Also, with that said, there is the idea that one's system of reference can only be found outside of Western society (in the Sharia and the umma, the world Islamic community). A third group with a more traditionalist orientation tends to withdraw from society without at all wanting to participate. If these characteristically traditional believers fall into the hands of radical preachers or more specifically experience a type of 'awakening' to 'true' Islam and are indoctrinated in an extremist milieu, then the step to radicalism can be short. On the basis of the diverse factors which can lead an individual to slip into extremism, the latent potential for a politico-religiously motivated radicalization in Germany, as the study emphasizes, cannot be reliably estimated. However, on the basis of the available investigation, the authors assume an amount of approximately 10-12% of the Muslims in Germany, which would mean an order of magnitude of between 320,000 and 420,000 people.

Over 90% of people reject killing people in the name of God as not justifiable, and likewise over 90% of people consider a person who "*calls upon young Muslims to commit suicide attacks or leads them to do so*" to be a "*Godless criminal.*" On the other hand, about 44% of people agree either 'completely' or 'rather' with the statement "*Muslims who die for the faith through armed battle* [enter] *into paradise*," i.e., are rewarded by God for their acts. "Just under 40% consider that "*the use of physical violence as a reaction to threats to Islam by the West is legitimate.*" There are almost 10% who advocate using Sharia punishment in Germany – which in absolute terms

---

[75] Wolfgang Ritsch came to this result as early as 1987, for example: *Die Rolle des Islams für die Koranschulerziehung in der Bundesrepublik Deutschland. Hochschulschriften 244*, Pahl-Rugenstein: Köln, 1987.

means a number over 300,000 people. About a quarter of youth answers in the affirmative when it comes to preparedness to turn to physical violence against unbelievers in the service of the Islamic community. Anyway, there are just over 10% of youth who also answer in the affirmative regarding the justification of corporal punishment in Germany.

The study clearly indicates further – and here the comparison between preparatory high school students and university students is particularly significant – that a well-founded education is a factor which makes a development towards radicalization more improbable. Simultaneously, education does not automatically exclude radicalization, which the statements of student groups and their sometimes strong rejection of the Western lifestyle and social order especially show. Consequently, it is correct to emphasize the importance of education, since in the higher educational segment a smaller proportion countenance politico-religiously motivated violence. On the other hand, it is also clear that radicalism is not only to be combated with education and enlightenment alone. Rather, it is the ideology of radicalization which constitutes the actual problem: Among individuals who are students, the authors of the study find that the portion of those who on the basis of their distance to democracy and Western society, their rigid religious attitudes, and their disdain for other religions, are subject to a latent radicalization danger is estimated to be the enormously high level of 30%. Among the general population, the portion is higher still: *"Fundamental orientation, which links tight religious engagement, high everyday relevance of religion, strong focus on religious rules and rituals with the tendency to ostracize Muslims who do not follow them, along with granting enhanced status to Islam in a wholesale manner and to denigrating cultures which are Western and characterized by Christianity, is an attitude demonstrating a broad degree of dissemination. Among the general population one can ascribe such an orientation to about 40% of all people."*[76]

Moreover, the study brings to light that there are still very many third generation Muslims who do not look at themselves as German. This can also be the case where German citizenship has long since been received. 57% are either 'poorly integrated' or at best 'moderately integrated'. Only around 12% are well or very well integrated. An alarming fact to mention in this connection is that just under one-half of the Muslim residential population feels snubbed by the German population. This feeling receives a negative confirmation due to the fact that almost 20% of non-Muslim youth experience de-

---

[76] *Muslims in Germany*. A study by the Federal Ministry of the Interior on Integration, Barriers to Integration, Religion and Attitudes Toward Democracy, the Constitutional State, and Politically and Religiously Motivated Violence. Results of Surveys Within the Framework of a Multicentric Study in Urban Environments, by Kathrin Brettfeld and Peter Wetzels, 509 pp., Hamburg, 2007, p. 493. Also comp. my summary at http://www.gknd.de/Dokumente/030-Publikationen/033-Sachbeitraege/SB-2008-05-22.pdf (February 16, 2009).

cidedly xenophobic attitudes. Therein lies the substantiation for exceptional conflict potential with respect to the future coexistence of Muslims and non-Muslims.

With respect to the Sharia in Germany, neither panic nor belittlement is appropriate. Solid information and fact-based critical thinking as well as deepened engagement with the material must take the top position. This will help in countering those who are pursuing a politico-Islamic agenda and also support those who advocate the unreserved recognition of local (European) legal norms, those Muslims who have successfully managed to integrate into European society, and those who promote the educational and integration progress of their fellow countrymen and fellow believers. The implicit nature of a proper level of self-awareness with regard to one's own identity was something which was too little pronounced for far too long. Likewise, the goal-oriented involvement of the majority of Muslims who are apolitical in the present discussion, with the objective of encouraging them to identify with Western societies, has also not been characteristic. In times when Islam is gaining strength globally, the discussion and controversy surrounding the Sharia will not pass by Germany. The discussion has to be led by experts who resist the Sharia's political claim on Europe and who justifiably defend sole recognition of local law.

Literature

General Information about Islam

The most comprehensive collections of 'hadith':
> http://www.usc.edu/dept/MSA/fundamentals/hadithsunnah/

www.quran.org.uk

www.msawest.net/islam/

www.islam.tc/ask-imam/index.php

Karen Armstrong. *Islam: A Short History.* New York, 2002.

Harry Gaylord Dorman. *Toward Understanding Islam.* New York, 1948.

F. E. Peters. *Muhammad and the Origins of Islam.* State University of New York Press: Albany 1994.

David Wainers. *An Introduction to Islam.* Cambridge, 1995.

In German:

Bobzin, Hartmut. *Der Koran.* C. H. Beck: München, 2007.

Bobzin, Hartmut. *Mohammed.* C. H. Beck: München, 2006/3.

Paret, Rudi. *Mohammed und der Koran.* Kohlhammer: Stuttgart, 1991/3.

Schirrmacher, Christine. *Der Islam. Geschichte, Lehre, Unterschiede zum Christentum.* Hänssler: Holzgerlingen, 2003/2.

Zirker, Hans. *Der Koran. Zugänge und Lesarten.* Primus: Darmstadt, 1999.

Information about the Sharia

The major sources and authors concerning Sharia are described and linked at:
> http://www.llrx.com/features/islamiclaw.htm

Islamic fatwas: http://www.fatwa-online.com/

Yusuf Abdallah al-Qaradawi. *The Lawful and the Prohibited in Islam.* Islamic Book Service: 1982.

Syed Ameer Ali. *Mahommedan Law.* 2 vols. Kitab Bhavan: New Dehli, 1986.

Noel Coulson. *A History of Islamic Law.* Edinburgh University Press: Edinburgh, 1994A.

Kevin Reinhart. Ethics and the Qur'an. in: Jane Dammen McAuliffe (Ed.). Encyclopaedia of the Qur'an, Vol. 2, E. J. Brill: Leiden, 2002, p. 55-79.

R. Doi. *Shari'ah: The Islamic Law.* London, 1984/1997.

Baudouin Dupret, Maurits Berger, Laila al-Zwaini. *Legal Pluralism in the Arab World.* Arab and Islamic Laws Series, vol. 18. Kluwer Law International: The Hague, 1999.

Wael B. Hallaq. *A History of Islamic Legal Theories.* An Introduction to Sunni Usul Al-Fiqh. Cambridge University Press: Cambridge, 1997.

Joseph Schacht. *An Introduction to Islamic Law.* Clarendon Press: Oxford, 1996.

Christine Schirrmacher. "Sharia – is Origins, is Content and is Significance for Europe." Islam and Christianity 10 (2010) 1:30-36.

Bernard G. Weiss. *The Spirit of Islamic Law*. The University of Georgia Press: Athens, Georgia, USA, 1998.

Muhammad Qasim Zaman. "Sin, Major and Minor" in *Encyclopaedia of the Qur'an*, Vol. V, E. J. Brill: Leiden, 2006, p. 19-28.

In German:

El Baradie, Adel. *Gottes-Recht und Menschenrecht. Grundlagenprobleme der islamischen Strafrechtslehre*. Nomos: Baden-Baden, 1983.

Heller, Erdmute; Mosbahi, Hassouna (Hg.). *Islam, Demokratie, Moderne. Aktuelle Antworten arabischer Denker*. C. H. Beck: München, 1998.

Internationale Gesellschaft für Menschenrechte (IGFM), Frankfurt zur Scharia: http://www.igfm.de/?id=437 (Informationen zu Steinigung und Apostasiestrafen).

Nagel, Tilman. *Das islamische Recht. Eine Einführung*. WVA-Verlag Skulima: Westhofen, 2001.

Tellenbach, Silvia. *Strafgesetze der Islamischen Republik Iran*. Walter de Gruyter: Berlin, 1996. (eine Übersetzung des iranischen Strafgesetzbuches)

Tibi, Bassam. *Im Schatten Allahs. Der Islam und die Menschenrechte*. Piper: München, 1994.

Information about Islamic Politics

Tahir Abbas. *Islamic Radicalism and Multicultural Politics: The British Experience*. Routledge: New York, 2010.

Riaz Ahmed. The Concept of the Islamic State as Found in the Writings of Abul A' La Maudūdī. Durham: Diss., 1969.

Rudolph Peters. *Jihad in Classical and Modern Islam*. Marcus Wiener Publ.: Princeton,NY, 1996.

Christine Schirrmacher. *Islam and Society.* Global Issues Series 5. Bonn, 2009, download at http://iirf.eu/index.php?id=257&L=%271

Mariz Tadros, Akram Habib. *The Muslim Brotherhood and Islamist Politics in the Middle East*. Routledge: London, 2008.

William Montgomery Watt. Islamic *Fundamentalism and Modernity.* Routledge: London, 1988.

Information about Women in Islam

Leila Ahmed, *Women and Gender in Islam: Historical roots of a modern debate*. Yale University Press, 1992.

Engineer, Ashgar Ali. *The Rights of Women in Islam.* C. Hurst & Company: London, 1992 (eine eher liberale Ansicht).

John L. Esposito. *Women in Muslim Family Law*. Syracuse University Press: Syracuse/Ny, 1982

Yvonne Haddad and John Esposito. *Islam, Gender, and Social Change*, Published 1998. Oxford University Press.

Chibli Mallat; Jane Connors (eds.). *Islamic Family Law*. Graham & Trotman: London, 1993

Suad Joseph and Afsaneh Najmabadi. *Encyclopedia of Women & Islamic Cultures*. 5 volumes. Leiden: E. J. Brill, 2005.

Lynn Welchman. *Beyond the Code*: *Muslim Family Law and the Shari'a Judiciary in the Palestinian West Bank.* Kluwer Law Int.: The Hague, 2000.

In German:

El-Bahnassawi, Salim. *Die Stellung der Frau zwischen Islam und weltlicher Gesetzgebung. SKD Bavaria* Verlag: München, 1993 (vermittelt die sehr traditionelle islamische Sichtweise).

Breuer, Rita. *Familienleben im Islam. Traditionen, Konflikte, Vorurteile.* Herder: Freiburg, 2002/4.

Schirrmacher, Christine. *Kleines Lexikon zur islamischen Familie.* Hänssler: Holzgerlingen, 2002.

Ursula Spuler-Stegemann; Christine Schirrmacher. *Frauen und die Scharia.* Hugendubel: München, 2004 (eine Erläuterung des islamischen Ehe- und Familienrechts).

Jag Jivan, Jennifer. „Im Namen der Ehre" in *Länderheft Pakistan.* Evangelisches Missionswerk in Deutschland (EMW): Hamburg, 2002, S. 141-148.

Information about Honor Killing

L. Abu-Odeh. "Crimes of Honour and the Construction of Gender in Arab Society" in M. Yamani (Hg.). *Feminism and Islam.* London: 1996, 141-194.

Amnesty International (Hg.), Pakistan. "Honour killings of girls and women"(1999), web.amnesty.org/library/print/ENGASA330181999.

Chesler, Phyllis, 2009, "Are Honor Killings Simply Domestic Violence?" Middle East Quarterly XVI(2): 61-69.

Yotam Feldner. "«Honour» murders – Why the perps get off easy" (sic), in MEQ 2000, 41-50. (www.meforum.org/article/50, 1-8).

Sohail Warraic. "'Honour Killings' and the Law in Pakistan," Chapter 4 of *Honour, Crimes, paradigms, and violence against women.* ed. by Sara Hossain and Lynn Welchman, Zed Books, 2005.

In German:

Böhmecke, Myria. *Tatmotiv Ehre.* Schriftenreihe NEIN zu Gewalt an Frauen, Terre desFemmes. (Hg.), Tübingen 2004

Gashi, Hanife. *Mein Schmerz trägt Deinen Namen. Ein Ehrenmord in Deutschland,* Hamburg 2005

Internationales Zentrum für Menschenrechte der Kurden IMK e. V. (Hg.), „Mord im Namen der Ehre". Entwicklungen und Hintergründe von „Ehrenmorden", Bonn 2003

Schirrmacher, Christine. „Mord im Namen der ‚Ehre' zwischen Migration und Tradition." Rechtspolitisches Forum – Legal Policy Forum 37. Trier: Institut für Rechtspolitik an der Universität Trier, 2007.

Information about Human Rights in Islam

"Cairo Declaration on Human Rights in Islam".
http://www1.umn.edu/humanrts/instree/cairodeclaration.html

"Universal Human Rights and Human Rights in Islam".
http://www.dhimmitude.org/archive/universal_islam.html.

Kazemi, Farouh. "Perspectives on Islam and Civil Society" in *Islamic Political Ethics: Civil Society, Pluralism and Conflict,* Sohail H. Hashmi, ed. Princeton University Press, 2002.

Ann Elizabeth Mayer. *Islam and Human Rights. Tradition and Politics.* West View Press: Boulder et.al., 1999/4.

In German:

Bielefeldt, Heiner. *Menschenrechte in der islamischen Diskussion.* http://www.kompetenz-interkulturell.de/userfiles/Grundsatzartikel/Menschenrechte%20Islam.pdf?SID=0c78d056429965b651a59ae0c9ab957c.

Duncker, Anne. *Menschenrechte im Islam. Eine Analyse islamischer Erklärungen über die Menschenrechte.* Wissenschaftlicher Verlag: Berlin, 2006.

Hofmann, Murad. *Der Islam und die Menschenrechte.* http://www.way-to-allah.com/themen/Menschenrechte.html.

Jürgensen, Carsten. *Demokratie und Menschenrechte in der arabischen Welt. Positionen arabischer Menschenrechtsaktivisten.* Deutsches Orient-Institut: Hamburg, 1994.

„Kairoer Erklärung der Menschenrechte" in Gewissen und Freiheit, Nr. 36/1991 und: http://www.aidlr.org/german/mag/36_1%20-5.pdf.

Müller, Lorenz. *Islam und Menschenrechte. Sunnitische Muslime zwischen Islamismus, Säkularismus und Modernismus.* Deutsches Orient-Institut: Hamburg, 1996.

Schirrmacher, Christine. *Islamische Menschenrechtserklärungen und ihre Kritiker. Einwände von Muslimen und Nichtmuslimen gegen die Allgültigkeit der Scharia.* Vortrag im Rahmen der Tagung "Sharia and Western Legal Systems" des „Instituts für Rechtspolitik (IRP) an der Universität Trier, 31.10.2006 (im Erscheinen begriffen).

Information about Renouncing Islam

http://en.wikipedia.org/wiki/Apostasy_in_Islam.

Ahmad, Mirza Tahir. *Murder in the Name of Allah.* Guildford: Lutterworth Press, 1968

Mawdudi, Abul Ala. "The Punishment of the Apostate according to Islamic Law." o. O. 1994.

Peters, Rudolph; de Vries, Gert J. J.. "Apostasy in Islam" in *Welt des Islam* 17/1976-77, S. 1-25. doi:10.1163/157006076X00017.

Rahman, S. A. *Punishment of Apostasy in Islam.* Institute of Islamic Culture: Lahore, 1972

Ibn Warraq. *Leaving Islam: Apostates speak out.* Prometheus Books: Amhurst/NY, 2003, 89-100+277-292+365-368.

In German:

Hauser, Albrecht (Hg.) *Christen in islamischen Ländern. Veröffentlicht durch das Referat Mission,* Ökumene und kirchlicher Entwicklungsdienst des Evangelischen Oberkirchenrats Stuttgart, Imatel: Stuttgart (1993).

Khoury, Adel Theodor. *Christen unterm Halbmond. Religiöse Minderheiten unter der Herrschaft des Islam.* Herder: Freiburg, 1994.

Khoury, Adel Theodor; Hagemann, Ludwig. *Christentum und Christen im Denken zeitgenössischer Muslime.* CIS-Verlag: Altenberge, 1986.

About the Author

Published by the Author

Books by Christine Schirrmacher

Mit den Waffen des Gegners. Christlich-Muslimische Kontroversen im 19. und 20. Jahrhundert, dargestellt am Beispiel der Auseinandersetzung um Karl Gottlieb Pfanders 'mìzân al-haqq' und Rahmatullâh Ibn Halìl al-'Utmânì al-Kairânawìs 'izhâr al-haqq' und der Diskussion über das Barnabasevangelium. Islamkundliche Untersuchungen 162. Klaus Schwarz Verlag: Berlin, 1992 *(Dissertation, Part 1: Christian missionary and Muslim apologetical literature of 19th and 20th century; Part 2: history of the "Gospel of Barnabas", a forgery of the Middle Ages, serving as a "proof" to argue against Christianity)*

Der Islam: Geschichte – Lehre – Unterschiede zum Christentum. 2 vols. Hänssler: Neuhausen, 1994/20032 *(Islam – history, dogmatics, ethics, Sharia law, political Islam, detailed comparison of Islam and Christianity)*

The Islamic View of Major Christian Teachings. RVB: Hamburg, 2001[1]; The WEA Global Issues Series, Vol. 2. VKW: Bonn, 2008[2]

La Vision Islamica de Importantes Ensenanzas Cristianas (Spanish Translation of: The Islamic View of Major Christian Teachings). Funad: Nicaragua, 2002[1]; RVB International: Hamburg, 2003[2]

Herausforderung Islam – Der Islam zwischen Krieg und Frieden. Hänssler: Holzgerlingen, 2002 *(Is Islam a religion of peace? What does Jihad mean?)*

Kleines Lexikon der islamischen Familie. Hänssler: Holzgerlingen, 2002 *(Muslim family law and family values)*

„Lexikon des Islam", S. 428-549 in: Thomas Schirrmacher, Christine Schirrmacher u. a. Harenberg Lexikon der Religionen. Harenberg Verlag: Düsseldorf, 2002 *(Major dictionary on world religions)*

(with Ursula Spuler-Stegemann) Frauen und die Scharia: Die Menschenrechte im Islam. München: Hugendubel, 2004 *(Women under the Sharia – Human rights in Islam)*

Der Islam – Eine Einführung. St. Johannis Druckerei: Lahr, 2005 *(Short Introduction into Islam)*

Islam und Christlicher Glaube – ein Vergleich. Hänssler: Holzgerlingen, 2006 *(Islam and Christianity compared)*

Mord im „Namen der Ehre" zwischen Migration und Tradition. Institut für Rechtspolitik an der Universität Trier: Trier, 2007 *(Study on Honour killings, published by State University of Trier)*

Islamische Menschenrechtserklärungen und ihre Kritiker. Einwände von Muslimen und Nichtmuslimen gegen die Allgültigkeit der Scharia. Institut für Rechtspolitik an der Universität Trier: Trier, 2007 *(Muslim Human Rights Declarations and Sharia law, published by State University of Trier)*

Die Scharia – Recht und Gesetz im Islam. Hänssler: Holzgerlingen, 2008 *(Sharia – Law and Order in Islam)*

Islam and Society: Sharia Law – Jihad – Women in Islam. The WEA Global Issues Series, Vol. 4. VKW: Bonn, 2008

Islamismus: Wenn Religion zur Politik wird. SCM Hänssler: Holzgerlingen, 2010 *(Islamism – When Faith turns out to be Politics)*

i-seul-lam-ui gwan-jeom hak-seup-ha-gi: i-seul-lam-gwa gi-dok-gyo gyo-ui (Korean Translation of: The Islamic View of Major Christian Teachings). Translated by Dae Ok Kim · Byeong Hei Jun. Doseochulpan Baul: Incheon Metropolitan City, Korea, 2010

i-seul-lam-gwa sa-hoe: i-seul-lam beob – ji-ha-d – i-seul-lam-ui yeo-seong (Korean Translation of Islam and Society: Sharia Law – Jihad – Women in Islam). Translated by Dae Ok Kim · Byeong Hei Jun. Doseochulpan Baul: Incheon Metropolitan City, Korea, 2011

Islam – An Introduction (English Translation of: Der Islam – Eine Einführung). The WEA Global Issues Series Vol. 6. VKW: Bonn, 2011

Mtazamo wa Uislamu juu ya Mafundisho Makuu ya Ukristo: Jukumu la Yesu Kristo Dhambi, Imani na Msamaha (Kiswahili Translation of The Islamic View of Major Christian Teachings:). TASCM: Mwanza (Tanzania) & RVB: Hamburg, 2012

Die Frage der Freiwilligkeit der islamischen Eheschließung. Rechtspolitisches Forum – Legal Policy Forum 61. Trier: Institut für Rechtspolitik an der Universität Trier, 2012 *(What does Islam teach about forced marriages)?*

Islam und Demokratie: Ein Gegensatz? SCM Hänssler: Holzgerlingen, 2013 *(Islam and Democracy – An Antagonism?)*

Sharia – Law and Order in Islam (English Translation of: Die Sharia – Recht und Gesetz im Islam). The WEA Global Issues Series Vol. 10. VKW: Bonn, 2013

Perspectiva Islamului asupra principalelor învățături creștine (Romanian Translation of: The Islamic View of Major Christian Teachings). The WEA Global Issues Series Vol. 2. VKW: Bonn, 2013

Political Islam – When Faith turns out to be Politics (English Translation of: Islamismus – Wenn Glaube zu Politik wird). The WEA Global Issues Series. VKW: Bonn, 2013

Islam and Democracy – An Antagonism? (English Translation of: Islam und Demokratie: Ein Gegensatz?). The WEA Global Issues Series (upcoming 2013)

"There is no Compulsion in Religion" (Surah 2: 256). Contemporary influential Muslim theologians on Apostasy. Yusuf al-Qaradawi, Abdullah Saeed and Abu l-A'la Maududi on Religious Freedom, Human Rights and Apostasy (upcoming 2013)

Recent articles by Christine Schirrmacher (selection)

"Muslim Apologetics and the Agra Debates of 1854: A Nineteenth Century Turning Point". The Bulletin of the Henry Martyn Institute of Islamic Studies 13 (1994) 1/2 (Jan-Jun): 74-84 (Hyderabad, Indien)

"The Fall of Man and Redemption of Mankind – What Does the Qur'an Teach?". Reflection: An International Reformed Review of Missiology 5 (1994/1995): 3/4 (March/May): 17-22

"The Crucifixion of Jesus in View of Muslim Theology". Reflection: An International Reformed Review of Missiology 5 (1994/1995): 3/4 (March/May): 23-29

"La Bible et le Coran Comparés". La Revue Reformee 48 (1997) 3: 25-30

"The Influence of Higher Bible Criticism on Muslim Apologetics in the Nineteenth Century". pp. 270-279 in: Jacques Waardenburg (Ed). Muslim Perceptions of Other Religions. Oxford University Press: New York/Oxford, 1999

"How Muslims View Christians: Part 1". Islam and Christianity 0 (2000) 1: 8-12

"How Muslims View Christians: Part 2". Islam and Christianity 1 (2001) 1: 12-17

"Steps to effective 'Dawah' – Practical Instructions for the Muslim 'Missionary'". Islam and Christianity 3 (2003) 1: 33-36

"Human Rights and the Persecution of Christians in Islam". pp. 119-126 in: Thomas Schirrmacher (Ed.). A Life of Transformation: From Politician to Good Samaritan: A Festschrift for Colonel V. Doner. RVB: Hamburg, 2002

„Frauen unter der Scharia". Aus Politik und Zeitgeschichte B 48/2004, pp. 10-16 (Beilage zu Das Parlament 22.11.2004) *(Women under Sharia, published by the Federal Parliament of Germany)*

"Suicide, Martyrdom and Jihad in the Koran, Islamic Theology and Society". Islam and Christianity 4 (2004) 1: 10-14

"Shiite Ashura Ceremonies: Redemption through Penitence and Suffering". Islam und Christlicher Glaube / Islam and Christianity 5 (2005) 2: 23-25

"Taqiya – The Dictate of Secrecy in Emergency". Islam und Christlicher Glaube / Islam and Christianity 5 (2005) 2: 28-29

"Shiite Theologians: Ayatollah Khomeini (1902-1989)". Islam und Christlicher Glaube / Islam and Christianity 5 (2005) 2: 33-35

„Der Islam über den Frieden, den Jihad und das Zusammenleben von Muslimen und Nichtmuslimen". Lutherische Nachrichten 26 (2006) 1, pp. 33-55 *(Islamic perspectives on the peaceful coexistence of different religions)*

"Honor killings und Ideas of Honor in Societies of Islamic Character". Islam and Christianity 6 (2006) 2: 30-35

„Rechtsvorstellungen im Islam". pp. 339-364 in: Horst Dreier, Eric Hilgendorf (Ed.). Kulturelle Identität als Grund und Grenze des Rechts: Akten der IVR-Tagung vom 28.-30. September 2006 in Würzburg. Nomos: Stuttgart, 2008 *(Development and practical application of Sharia law, published by State University of Würzburg)*

„Islam und Säkularisierung: Dargestellt am Beispiel islamischer Menschenrechtserklärungen". pp. 363-406 in: Walter Schweidler (Ed.). Postsäkulare Gesellschaft: Perspektiven interdisziplinärer Forschung. Verlag Karl Alber: München, 2007 *(Is a Secularization of Sharia law possible?)*

„Herausforderung Islam". pp. 264-278 in: Hans Zehetmaier (Ed.). Politik aus christlicher Verantwortung. Hanns Seidel Stiftung & Verlag für Sozialwissenschaften: Wiesbaden, 2007 *(The challenge of Islam in Germany)*

„Islam und Christentum in Europa: Eine Standortbestimmung". pp. 145-162 in: Lutz Simon, Hans-Joachim Hahn (Ed.). Europa ohne Gott: Auf der Suche nach unserer kulturellen Identität. Hänssler: Holzgerlingen, 2007 *(What is Europe's culturally and religiously defined identity?)*

„Der Islam über den Frieden, den Jihad und das Zusammenleben von Muslimen und Nichtmuslimen". pp. 259-276 in: Reinhard Hempelmann, Johannes Kandel (Ed.). Religionen und Gewalt. V&R unipress: Göttingen, 2006 *(Teachings of Islam about jihad and martyrdom)*

„Christen im Urteil von Muslimen: Kritische Positionen aus der Frühzeit des Islam und aus der Sicht heutiger Theologen". pp. 12-34 in: Ursula Spuler-Stegemann. Feindbild Christentum im Islam. Bonn: Bundeszentrale für politische Bildung, 2006 (Lizenzausgabe von 2004[2]) *(The Islamic view of Christians and Christianity since the early days of Islam, re-published by the Federal government)*

„Heterogen und kontrovers: Die innerislamische Debatte zum Thema Menschenrechte". pp. 273-294 in: Hamid Reza Yousefi u. a. (Ed.). Wege zu Menschenrechten. Traugott Bautz: Nordhausen, 2008 *(Islamic Human Rights Declarations and their critics)*

„Muslime in Deutschland: Ergebnisse der Studie – Eine Zusammenfassung". Gesprächskreis Nachrichtendienste in Deutschland e. V. – Mitgliederinformation 001/2208 (11.2.2008), Berlin, 2008 *(Summary of a detailed study about Muslims in Germany, condudcted by Federal Minister of the Interior)*

"Muslim Immigration to Europe and Its Challenge for European Societies". pp. 653-667: William Dembski, Thomas Schirrmacher (Edd.). Tough-Minded Christianity: Honoring the Legacy of John Warwick Montgomery. B&H Academic Publ.: Nashville (TN), 2009

„Ehrenmord und Emanzipation: Geschlechterrollen in Migrantenkulturen vor dem Hintergrund nahöstlicher Begriffe von ‚Ehre' und ‚Schande'". pp. 11-30 in: Bernhard Heininger. Ehrenmord und Emanzipation: Die Geschlechterfrage in Ritualen von Parallelgesellschaften. Geschlecht – Symbol – Religion 6. Lit Verlag: Berlin, 2009 *(About concepts of honour and shame in Islamic cultures and honour killings)*

"Defection from Islam: A Disturbing Human Rights Dilemma". International Journal for Religious Freedom (Cape Town) 3 (2010) 2: 13-38

"Sharia – its Origins, its Content and its Significance for Europe". Islam and Christianity 10 (2010) 1: 30-36

"Defection from Islam: A Disturbing Human Rights Dilemma". International Journal for Religious Freedom (Cape Town) 3 (2010) 2: 13-38

„Konvertiten zum Islam: Je gläubiger – je radikaler?". pp. 133-149: Reinhard Hempelmann (Ed.). Religionsdifferenzen und Religionsdialoge: Festschrift – 50 Jahre EZW. Berlin: Evangelische Zentralstelle für Weltanschauungsfragen, 2010 *(On the radicalization of Muslims in Germany)*

"Silenced: How Apostasy and Blasphemy Codes are Choking Freedom Worldwide, Paul Marshall, Nina Shea" (Review). International Journal for Religious Freedom (Cape Town) 5 (2012) 2: 169-171

„50 Jahre Islam in Deutschland – Ist seine ‚Anerkennung' durch den deutschen Staat überfällig?". pp. 99-109 in: Philipp W. Hildmann, Stefan Rößle (Edd.). Staat und Kirche im 21. Jahrhundert. Berichte & Studien 96. München: Hanns-Seidel-Stiftung, 2012 *(Is an official recognition of Islam as a religious body by the German state overdue?)*

„Die Rolle des Islamismus bei der Arabischen Revolution: Eine Momentaufnahme". pp. 79-94 in: Österreichisches Studienzentrum für Frieden und Konfliktforschung, Bert Preiss (Ed.). Zeitenwende im arabischen Raum: Welche Antwort findet Europa? Wien: LIT, 2012 *(The role of political Islam during the Arab Revolutions/the Arab Spring)*

„Geistesgeschichtliche Ursprünge des Politischen Islam / Islamismus". pp. 5-11 in: Johannes Kandel; Politische Akademie der Friedrich-Ebert-Stiftung (Edd.). ‚Politischer Islam' – ‚Islamismus': Extremistische Islam-Varianten in der Diskussion 20.-22. Oktober 2011. Berlin Forum for Progressive Muslims. Berlin: Friedrich Ebert Stiftung, 2012. www.fes.de/cgi-bin/gbv.cgi?id=09185&ty=pdf *(On the origins of Political Islam/Islamism)*

"The Relationship between Islam and Democracy". Islam and Christianity 13 (2013) 1: 13-20

Biography

Prof. Dr. Christine Schirrmacher is a well-known international scholar of Islamic Studies, currently teaching at the Evangelisch-Theologische Faculteit (ETF) (Protestant University) at Leuven, Belgium, the department of Islamic Studies and the department of political science and sociology at the State University of Bonn, Germany.

She holds an M. A. and a PhD in Islamic Studies. Her doctoral dissertation dealt with the Muslim-Christian controversy in the 19th and 20th century, her thesis for her postdoctoral lecture qualification ("Habilitation") focused on contemporary Muslim theological voices on apostasy.

She regularly lectures on Islam and security issues at different government institutions of security policy in Germany. She also teaches at the Academy of Foreign Affairs of the Foreign Office in Berlin, and is a consultant to different advisory bodies of society and politics, e. g. to the Human Rights Committee of the „Bundestag", i. e. the German federal parliament.

She is director of the International Institute of Islamic Studies (IIIS) of the World Evangelical Alliance (WEA) and its regional counterpart, the „Institut für Islamfragen" (Institute of Islamic Studies) of the German, Swiss and Austrian Evangelical Alliance, as well as speaker and advisor on Islam for WEA.

She is member of the „Gesprächskreis Nachrichtendienste, Berlin" (Intelligence Discussion group), of the International Society for Human Rights, of the „Deutsch-Jordanische Gesellschaft" (German-Jordanian Society) and curatorium member of the „Evangelische Zentralstelle für Weltanschauungsfragen" (Protestant Centre for World View Questions), an academic documentation and advisory centre of the Protestant Church of Germany.

She has visited many Muslim majority countries of the Near and Middle East, and has been speaker at national as well as international conferences dealing with Islam, held by non-religious, Christian and Muslim organisations.

She is engaged in current dialogue initiatives, like the conference "Loving God and Neighbour in Word and Deed: Implications for Muslims and Christians" of the Yale Centre for Faith and Culture, Yale University, New Haven, 2008 or the "Berlin Forum for Progressive Muslims" of the Friedrich-Ebert-Stiftung, 2011/2013.

She has widely published on the subjects of islamism, jihadism and political Islam, on Islam and democracy, on women in Islamic societies, on sharia law, on human rights in Islam and on integration and radicalization of Muslims in Europe. Besides many scholarly articles, she published 15 books in German, translated into English, Spanish, Kiswahili, Romanian and Korean.

Her two volume introduction „Der Islam – Geschichte, Lehre, Unterschiede zum Christentum" (1994/2003) (*Islam – History, Dogmatics, Differences to Christianity*) is widely used in education. Among her recent books are „Frauen und die Scharia – Die Menschenrechte im Islam" (2004/2006) (*Women and Sharia Law - Human Rights in Islam*), „Der Islam – eine Einführung" (2005) (*Islam – A Short Introduction*), „Die Scharia – Recht und Gesetz im Islam" (2008) (*The Sharia – Law and Order in Islam*), „Islamismus – Wenn Glaube zur Politik wird" (2010) (*Islamism – When Faith turns out to be Politics)*, and „Islam und Demokratie – ein Gegensatz?" (2013) *(Islam and Democracy – an Antagonism?)*.

World Evangelical Alliance

World Evangelical Alliance is a global ministry working with local churches around the world to join in common concern to live and proclaim the Good News of Jesus in their communities. WEA is a network of churches in 129 nations that have each formed an evangelical alliance and over 100 international organizations joining together to give a worldwide identity, voice and platform to more than 600 million evangelical Christians. Seeking holiness, justice and renewal at every level of society – individual, family, community and culture, God is glorified and the nations of the earth are forever transformed.

Christians from ten countries met in London in 1846 for the purpose of launching, in their own words, "a new thing in church history, a definite organization for the expression of unity amongst Christian individuals belonging to different churches." This was the beginning of a vision that was fulfilled in 1951 when believers from 21 countries officially formed the World Evangelical Fellowship. Today, 150 years after the London gathering, WEA is a dynamic global structure for unity and action that embraces 600 million evangelicals in 129 countries. It is a unity based on the historic Christian faith expressed in the evangelical tradition. And it looks to the future with vision to accomplish God's purposes in discipling the nations for Jesus Christ.

Commissions:

- Theology
- Missions
- Religious Liberty
- Women's Concerns
- Youth
- Information Technology

Initiatives and Activities

- Ambassador for Human Rights
- Ambassador for Refugees
- Creation Care Task Force
- Global Generosity Network
- International Institute for Religious Freedom
- International Institute for Islamic Studies
- Leadership Institute
- Micah Challenge
- Global Human Trafficking Task Force
- Peace and Reconciliation Initiative
- UN-Team

Church Street Station
P.O. Box 3402
New York, NY 10008-3402
Phone +[1] 212 233 3046
Fax +[1] 646-957-9218
www.worldea.org

International Institute for Religious Freedom

Purpose and Aim

The "International Institute for Religious Freedom" (IIRF) is a network of professors, researchers, academics, specialists and university institutions from all continents with the aim of working towards:

- The establishment of reliable facts on the restriction of religious freedom worldwide.
- The making available of results of such research to other researchers, politicians, advocates, as well as the media.
- The introduction of the subject of religious freedom into academic research and curricula.
- The backing up of advocacy for victims of violations of religious freedom in the religious, legal and political world.
- Serving discriminated and persecuted believers and academics wherever they are located. Publications and other research will be made available as economically and as readily available as possible to be affordable in the Global South.

Tools

The IIRF encourages all activities that contribute to the understanding of religious freedom. These include:

- Dissemination of existing literature, information about archives, compilation of bibliographies etc.
- Production and dissemination of new papers, journals and books.
- Gathering and analysis of statistics and evidence.
- Supplying of ideas and materials to universities and institutions of theological education to encourage the inclusion of religious freedom issues into curricula.
- Guiding postgraduate students in research projects either personally or in cooperation with the universities and educational institutions.
- Representation at key events where opportunity is given to strengthen connections with the wider religious liberty community and with politicians, diplomats and media.

Online / Contact:

- www.iirf.eu / info@iirf.eu

International Institute for Religious Freedom
Internationales Institut für Religionsfreiheit
Institut international pour la liber té religieuse
of the World Evangelical Alliance
Bonn – Cape Town – Colombo

Friedrichstr. 38	PO Box 535	32, Ebenezer Place
2nd Floor	Edgemead 7407	Dehiwela
53111 Bonn	Cape Town	(Colombo)
Germany	South Africa	Sri Lanka

Board of Supervisors
- *Chairman:* **Godfrey Yogarajah** (Sri Lanka)
- *Chairman emeritus:* Dr. Paul C. Murdoch
- Esme Bowers (South Africa)
- Julia Doxat-Purser (European Evangelical Alliance)
- John Langlois (World Evangelical Alliance)

Executives
- *Director:* **Prof. Dr. Dr. Thomas Schirrmacher** (Germany)
- *Co-Director:* **Prof. Dr. Christof Sauer** (South Africa)
- *Director Colombo Office:* **Roshini Wickremesinhe**, LLB (Sri Lanka)
- *CFO:* Manfred Feldmann (Germany)
- *Legal Counsel:* Martin Schweiger (Singapore)
- *Representative to UN, OSCE, EU:* Arie de Pater (Netherlands)
- *Senior research writer:* Fernando Perez (India)
- *Research Coordinator:* Joseph Yakubu (Nigeria)
- *Public relations:* Ron Kubsch (Germany)

Academic Board
with areas of research
- *Honorary Chairman:*
  Prof. Dr. Dr. John Warwick Montgomery (France)
- Tehmina Arora, LLB (India):
  Anti-conversion laws
- Prof. Dr. Janet Epp Buckingham (Canada):
  Human rights law
- Dr. Rosalee Velosso Ewell (Brazil):
  Consultations
- Prof. Dr. Lovell Fernandez (South Africa):
  Transitional justice
- Prof. Dr. Ken Gnanakan (India):
  Universities, Social justice
- Dr. Benyamin Intan (Indonesia):
  Peacebuilding
- Prof. Dr. Thomas Johnson (Czech Republic):
  Natural law ethics
- Max Klingberg (Germany):
  Human rights organizations
- Drs. Behnan Konutgan (Turkey):
  Orthodox Churches
- Dr. Paul Marshall (USA):
  Religious liberty research, Islam
- Patson Netha (Zimbabwe): Africa
- Ihsan Yinal Özbek (Turkey): Turkish Islam
- Prof. Glenn Penner † (Canada)
- Prof. Dr. Bernhard J. G. Reitsma (Netherlands): Islam and Christianity
- Prof. Dr. Christine Schirrmacher (Germany):
  Islamic Sharia
- Prof. Dr. Donald L. Stults (USA): Training
- Anneta Vyssotskaia (Russia):
  Central and Eastern Europe

The institute operates under the oversight of the World Evangelical Alliance and is registered as a company in Guernsey with its registered office at PO Box 265, Suite 6, Borough House, Rue du Pré, Saint Peter Port, Guernsey, Channel Islands, GY1 3QU.

The Colombo Bureau is registered with the Asia Evangelical Alliance, Sri Lanka.
The Cape Town Bureau is registered as 'IIRF Cape Town Bureau' in South Africa.
The Bonn Bureau is registered under ProMundis e. V. (Bonn, 20 AR 197/95)

Institute of Islamic Studies

The protestant "Institute of Islamic Studies" is a network of scholars in Islamic studies and is carried out by the Evangelical Alliance in Germany, Austria and Switzerland.

Churches, the political arena, and society at large are provided foundational information relating to the topic of 'Islam' through research and the presentation thereof via publications, adult education seminars, and democratic political discourse.

Research Focus

As far as our work is concerned, the focus is primarily on Islam in Europe, the global development of Islamic theology and of Islamic fundamentalism, as well as a respectful and issue-related meeting of Christians and Muslims. In the process, misunderstandings about Islam and Muslims can be cleared up, and problematic developments in Islamic fundamentalism and political Islam are explained. Through our work we want to contribute to engaging Muslims in an informed and fair manner.

What we do

Lectures, seminars, and conferences for public authorities, churches, political audiences, and society at large

- Participation in special conferences on the topic of Islam
- The publication of books in German, English, and Spanish
- The preparation of scholarly studies for the general public
- Special publications on current topics
- Production of a German-English journal entitled "Islam and Christianity"
- Regular press releases with commentaries on current events from a scholarly Islamic studies perspective
- Academic surveys and experts' reports for advisory boards of government
- Regular news provided as summaries of Turkish and Arab language internet publications
- Fatwa archive
- Website with a collection of articles

Islam and Christianity

Journal of the Institute of Islamic Studies and the International Institute of Islamic Studies

- German/English. All articles in both languages
- Topics of current issues: Women in Islam, Human Rights in Islam, Sharia law, Shii Islam.
- Editor: Prof. Dr. Christine Schirrmacher
  Executive Editor: Carsten Polanz
- ISSN 1616-8917
- 48 pp. twice annually
- 9,20 € per year including postage (airmail on request)
- **Sample copies and subscription**:
  Ifl · Pf 7427 · D-53074 Bonn · Germany
  info@islaminstitut.de
- **Download** under www.islaminstitut.de/zeitschrift.20.0.html

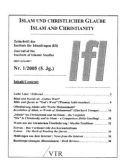

Institute for Islamic Studies (Ifl)
of the Evangelical Alliance in Germany, Austria, Switzerland

International Institute of Islamic Studies (IIIS)
of the World Evangelical Alliance

Ifl · Pf 7427 · D-53074 Bonn · Germany · info@islaminstitut.de

www.islaminstitute.net

Giving Hands

GIVING HANDS GERMANY (GH) was established in 1995 and is officially recognized as a nonprofit foreign aid organization. It is an international operating charity that – up to now – has been supporting projects in about 40 countries on four continents. In particular we care for orphans and street children. Our major focus is on Africa and Central America. GIVING HANDS always mainly provides assistance for self-help and furthers human rights thinking.

The charity itself is not bound to any church, but on the spot we are cooperating with churches of all denominations. Naturally we also cooperate with other charities as well as governmental organizations to provide assistance as effective as possible under the given circumstances.

The work of GIVING HANDS GERMANY is controlled by a supervisory board. Members of this board are Manfred Feldmann, Colonel V. Doner and Kathleen McCall. Dr. Christine Schirrmacher is registered as legal manager of GIVING HANDS at the local district court. The local office and work of the charity are coordinated by Rev. Horst J. Kreie as executive manager. Dr. theol. Thomas Schirrmacher serves as a special consultant for all projects.

Thanks to our international contacts companies and organizations from many countries time and again provide containers with gifts in kind which we send to the different destinations where these goods help to satisfy elementary needs. This statutory purpose is put into practice by granting nutrition, clothing, education, construction and maintenance of training centers at home and abroad, construction of wells and operation of water treatment systems, guidance for self-help and transportation of goods and gifts to areas and countries where needy people live.

GIVING HANDS has a publishing arm under the leadership of Titus Vogt, that publishes human rights and other books in English, Spanish, Swahili and other languages.

These aims are aspired to the glory of the Lord according to the basic Christian principles put down in the Holy Bible.

Baumschulallee 3a • D-53115 Bonn • Germany
Phone: +49 / 228 / 695531 • Fax +49 / 228 / 695532
www.gebende-haende.de • info@gebende-haende.de

Martin Bucer Seminary

Faithful to biblical truth
Cooperating with the Evangelical Alliance
Reformed

Solid training for the Kingdom of God
- Alternative theological education
- Study while serving a church or working another job
- Enables students to remain in their own churches
- Encourages independent thinking
- Learning from the growth of the universal church.

Academic
- For the Bachelor's degree: 180 Bologna-Credits
- For the Master's degree: 120 additional Credits
- Both old and new teaching methods: All day seminars, independent study, term papers, etc.

Our Orientation:
- Complete trust in the reliability of the Bible
- Building on reformation theology
- Based on the confession of the German Evangelical Alliance
- Open for innovations in the Kingdom of God

Our Emphasis:
- The Bible
- Ethics and Basic Theology
- Missions
- The Church

Our Style:
- Innovative
- Relevant to society
- International
- Research oriented
- Interdisciplinary

Structure
- 15 study centers in 7 countries with local partners
- 5 research institutes
- President: Prof. Dr. Thomas Schirrmacher
  Vice President: Prof. Dr. Thomas K. Johnson
- Deans: Thomas Kinker, Th.D.;
  Titus Vogt, lic. theol., Carsten Friedrich, M.Th.

Missions through research
- Institute for Religious Freedom
- Institute for Islamic Studies
- Institute for Life and Family Studies
- Institute for Crisis, Dying, and Grief Counseling
- Institute for Pastoral Care

www.bucer.eu • info@bucer.eu
Berlin | Bielefeld | Bonn | Chemnitz | Hamburg | Munich | Pforzheim
Innsbruck | Istanbul | Izmir | Linz | Prague | São Paulo | Tirana | Zurich